Spelling Success
in the Early Grades

**A Yearlong Plan to Teach Spelling Effectively in K-2:
Strategy Lessons, Guided Practice,
and Independent Activities**

By Eileen Hodrinsky, Debra McBride, Regina Moreno,
Pamela Sherman-Fowler, Tracey L. Varrone

NEW YORK • TORONTO • LONDON • AUCKLAND • SYDNEY
MEXICO CITY • NEW DELHI • HONG KONG • BUENOS AIRES

■SCHOLASTIC
Teaching
Resources

Dedications

To my loving family—Bill, Lori, and Jason—who encourage and continually inspire me; and to my parents, whose love and devotion were always the wind beneath my wings. —Eileen Hodrinsky

To my husband Janos, my daughter Miriam and my son Ben, and to our five grandchildren.

—Regina Moreno

To Chris, Noah, and Jonas, and to all of the wonderful teachers who have touched my career and inspired me to be the best teacher I can be. —Pam Sherman-Fowler

To Kevin and Andrew, for their love and understanding; and to Pat, whose strength and courage have been my inspiration. —Debra McBride

To my husband Peter and to my family, whose love and support inspire me every day. —Tracey Varrone

And a special dedication to all of the children who have touched our lives and to our colleagues, who have continually encouraged us.

Acknowledgments

Our sincere gratitude to all of the administrators, teachers, parents, and children in the Shoreham-Wading River School District who supported our pilot of this spelling/word study approach in primary classrooms.

Special thanks also to fellow educators in the Valley Stream Thirteen School District for their belief in our ideas and their enthusiastic adoption of our proposed instructional strategies.

Lastly, we must acknowledge the efforts of our visionary Scholastic editors, Wendy Murray, Joanna Davis-Swing, and Merryl Maleska Wilbur, and our talented designer Jackie Swensen, who had faith in our ideas, patiently guided our conceptualization of a clear format, and remained enthusiastically committed to our project.

This was truly a collegial effort that we are proud to share with our fellow educators and the learning community.

Credits

Finger-Spelling Alphabet illustrated by Maxie Chambliss

Spelling Word Study Strategy ("Look, Say, Copy, Cover and Write, Check") adapted from J. Richard Gentry, *Effective Practices for Spelling*, 2001, jrichardgentry.com

"Flashlights in the Dark" from *Perfect Poems for Teaching Phonics* by Frances Gorman Risser. Copyright © 1999 by Scholastic Inc. Reprinted with permission.

"Bugs" from *Thematic Poems, Songs, and Fingerplays* by Miesh Goldish. Copyright © 1994 by Scholastic Inc. Reprinted with permission.

"Seasons" and "Almost Lunchtime" from *A Poem a Day* by Helen H. Moore. Copyright © 1997 by Scholastic Inc. Reprinted with permission.

Excerpts from *Swing, Swing, Swing* by Gail Tuchman, illustrated by Shelley Dieterichs. Copyright © 1994 by Scholastic Inc. Reprinted with permission.

Excerpts from *We Like to Play* by Ellen Tarlow, illustrated by Luisa D'Augusta. Copyright © 2000 by Scholastic Inc. Reprinted with permission

Cover design by James Sarfati
Interior design by Solutions by Design, Inc.
Interior photos courtesy of the authors

ISBN 0-439-38530-X

1 2 3 4 5 6 7 8 9 10   40   09 08 07 06 05 04 03

CONTENTS

CHAPTER 1
Successful Spelling/Word Study Within a Balanced Literacy Program 7

A Year-Long Approach to Spelling/Word Study 8
Four Phases of Instruction 8
Key Elements and Features 9
Importance of Revisiting What's Been Learned 9

Strategy-Oriented Approach vs. Skill-Oriented Approach to Spelling Practices 10

Three Contexts for This Approach to Spelling/Word Study 10
Necessary Building Blocks for Good Spellers 10
Balanced Literacy Program 11
Gradual Release of Responsibility 12

The Weekly Picture: Components of the Approach 13
Explicit Teaching: Mini-Lessons 14
Guided Practice Activities 14
Independent Practice Activities 14
Home Links 17
Teacher Assessment of Student Learning 17

Making Spelling/Word Study Kid-Friendly 17

CHAPTER 2
Learning Sight Words: Visual and Auditory Sequencing Strategies 19
PHASE ONE: SEPTEMBER–OCTOBER

Explicit Teaching: Modeling Strategies Through Mini-lessons 20
Mini-Lesson #1: What Do Good Spellers Do? 21
Mini-Lesson #2: What Do Good Spellers Look at in Words? 22
Mini-Lesson #3: What Do Good Spellers Listen For? 23
Mini-Lesson #4: How Do Good Spellers Begin to Memorize Sight Words? 25
Mini-Lesson #5: How Do Good Spellers Study and Internalize the Spelling of Common Sight Words? . 26
Mini-Lesson #6: How Do Good Spellers Write Sight Words in Context? 27
Mini-Lesson #7: How Do Good Spellers Edit Their Writing? 28

Guided Practice Activities 28
Sky Writing 30
I Spy, Hear, & Say 30
Word Detectives 31
Word Sorts 33
Listen for the "Beat": Clapping Names 33
Sound Boxes 34
Sight Word Clues 35
Look, Say, Cover, Write, Check 36
Fast Eyes 37
Using Classroom Materials (Reference Tools) 38

    Independent Practice: Learning Center Activities 39
       Fun With Magnetic Letters 40
       Writing Words in Shaving Cream 41
       Go Fish Game 43
       Sight Word Puzzles 44
       Beans in a Can 44
       Sound Boxes 45

    Teacher Assessment of Student Learning 46
       Ongoing Assessment 46
       Specific Classroom-Based Assessments 47

CHAPTER 3

Developing Phonological Skills: Rhyming and Phoneme Manipulation 53

PHASE TWO: NOVEMBER–DECEMBER

    Explicit Teaching: Modeling Strategies Through Mini-Lessons 54
       Mini-Lesson #1: What Do Good Spellers Listen for in Texts? 55
       Mini-Lesson #2: What Do Good Spellers Look for in Rhyming Words? 56
       Mini-Lesson #3: How Do Good Spellers Build New Words? 57
       Mini-Lesson #4: How Else Do Good Spellers Edit Their Writing? 58

    Guided Practice Activities 59
       Fun With Songs, Poems, and Books 59
       Poem Detective 60
       Poem or Song/Word Play 61
       Song/Word Play 63
       Letter Cards 63
       Reference Tools: Class Chart 64

    Independent Practice: Learning Center Activities 66
       Listening for Rhymes in Poems and Songs 67
       Noticing Onset and Rime in Text 68
       Making New Rhymes 69
       Building New Words 69
       Change the Sound and Word Plays 70
       Using Rhythm Sticks to Recognize Word Parts 71
       Becoming Good Editors 72

    Teacher Assessment of Student Learning 73
       Ongoing Assessment 73
       Specific Classroom-Based Assessments 73

CHAPTER 4

Building Words: Using Visual, Auditory, and Meaning Features of Known Words to Make New Words 77

PHASE THREE: JANUARY–MARCH

    Explicit Teaching: Modeling Strategies Through Mini-Lessons 78
       Mini-Lesson #1: What Do Good Spellers Do to Build New Words? 79
       Mini-Lesson #2: How Else Do Good Spellers Build New Words? 79

Mini-Lesson #3: What Is Something Else Good Spellers Do to Build New Words?. 80
Mini-Lesson #4: What Else Do Good Spellers Use to Build New Words?. 81
Mini-Lesson #5: How Do Good Spellers Edit Their Writing?. 83

Guided Practice Activities 84
Pattern Sheets for Building on Known Words. 85
Discovering Parts of Compound Words 87
Pattern Sheets for Adding Suffixes and Prefixes to Known Words 88
Read Around the Room for Spelling Rule 1. 89
Read Around the Room for Spelling Rule 2. 90
Read Around the Room for Spelling Rules 3, 4, and 5 91
Reference Tools. 92

Independent Practice: Learning Center Activities 93
Building New Words. 94
Compound Word Puzzles 95
Adding Beginnings and Endings 96
Spelling Rule Games 97
Becoming Good Editors. 98

Assessment of Student Learning. 99
Ongoing Assessment 99
Specific Classroom-Based Assessments 100

CHAPTER 5
Making Connections: Using Common Word Families
(Phonograms or Rimes)

. . . . 103

PHASE FOUR: APRIL–JUNE

Explicit Teaching: Modeling Strategies Through Mini-Lessons 104
Mini-Lesson #1: What Do Good Spellers Do? 105
Mini-Lesson #2: How Do Good Spellers Build New Words? 106
Mini-Lesson #3: How Do Good Spellers Write New Words? 106
Mini-Lesson #4: How Do Good Spellers Edit Their Writing? 107

Guided Practice Activities 108
Word Family I Spy—Using Poems 108
Word Family Grids 109
Innovation on Text 109
Using Personal Dictionaries as a Reference Tool 110

Independent Practice: Learning Center Activities 111
Word Searches. 111
Word Wheels 112
Silly Sentences 113
Editing Word Family Text 114

Teacher Assessment of Student Learning 115
Ongoing Assessment 115
Specific Classroom-Based Assessments 115

Final Thoughts 117

Appendices 118

Introduction

Although the most current research in the field of literacy instruction is the theoretical basis for our spelling/word study approach, the impetus to change existing, habituated practices was sparked by a conversation with a precocious six-year-old. One evening in January 1998, friends came to visit. They entered our house laden with white cardboard bakery boxes, while their daughter Kelsey gripped her spelling homework journal and the stump of an over-sharpened pencil. As the adults began to chat, I watched Kelsey settle in on the couch and begin to complete the purple dittoed sheets neatly stapled into her black and white spelling journal. I glanced over at Kelsey and asked, "So, how's it going, Kelsey?"

"I hate doing spelling. This is so dumb!" she replied without hesitation.

"What do you have to do?"

"I have to put these words in alphabetical order and then fill in the blanks in these sentences. I already know which words to write, since the answers *have* to be one of my spelling words. Duh!"

Kelsey's mood was clear: she was bored and bothered by what she perceived as mindless activities that she was forced to complete in order "to become a good speller." First-grader Kelsey already found spelling to be a required drudgery. And I wondered what we well-intentioned educators were doing to our children.

I walked into our faculty room on Monday and shared Kelsey's story with my colleagues. We agreed that for years we teachers had approached spelling as a skill to be drilled and tested in an isolated format—such as the weekly spelling test—with little connection to actual writing or reading. We began to brainstorm how we could fashion a research-based, child-centered spelling/word study approach that would teach essential spelling skills and strategies, while simultaneously raising our students' spelling consciousness and fostering a positive attitude about word study. We revisited some popular spelling reinforcement activities, such as writing focus words three times each, alphabetizing lists of words, and then writing each spelling word in a complete sentence. Were these common classroom practices actually grounded in solid research, or simply passed on from one generation of teachers to another? From our own experience, we unanimously surmised that the latter was true.

We vowed that we owed it to our students to integrate research-proven spelling strategies into our authentic, literature-based classrooms. Working from a firm belief that spelling/word study should be an integral part of a Balanced Literacy Program (described in *The Teacher's Guide to the Four Block Multimethod, Multilevel Framework for Grades 1–3*, Cunningham, Hall, and Sigmon, 2001), we created and successfully field-tested a year-long approach to spelling/word study instruction. This approach began with students learning specific strategies for memorizing a core of basic sight words, then learning how to manipulate letters within known words to build new words, and ultimately using common letter patterns and key spelling rules to generate additional words.

This book is the result. It includes the five essential elements of our spelling/word study instructional approach: specific mini-lesson strategies for teachers to model; suggested materials and activities for guided practice; a plethora of ideas for classroom differentiated learning centers; ongoing assessment measures; and Home Links. These ideas were field-tested successfully in primary classrooms for three years.

The field-test results have been very exciting. Our students are developing the habits of proficient spellers, along with positive dispositions toward word study. Other teachers in various school districts throughout the United States and Canada have also been implementing this approach successfully. Parents have reported that, unlike my young friend Kelsey, their children now actually enjoy their home spelling assignments and understand why and how spelling is an important part of their overall word study. We wish you and your students success and enjoyment as you delve into this approach.

— *Eileen Hodrinsky, Gina Moreno, Pam Sherman-Fowler, Debra McBride, Tracey Varrone*

CHAPTER 1

Successful Spelling/Word Study Within a Balanced Literacy Program

We believe that learning to spell is about more than the memorization of weekly spelling words. We believe that it is—like speaking and reading—a process of figuring out language. In order to become a good speller, a child needs to have practice experimenting with language and seeing language. To that end, our goal in our own classrooms, as well as here in this book, is to offer creative ways for children to play naturally with language.

We recommend starting out by setting up a schedule that reflects the philosophy of a balanced literacy program. Practicing word study within the parameters of a balanced literacy program provides children with many opportunities to play with words, because word study is incorporated right into reading and writing instruction. Working within such an authentic learning environment means that you teach spelling strategies as they relate to a favorite book or poem you are reading in shared or guided reading, rather than in isolation.

In this chapter we provide a blueprint of how this approach fits into a full school year, as well as a more detailed look at the schedule for one week. We define the various components and give you a preview of what's to come. We also compare a traditional spelling skills approach to the more authentic strategies approach we advocate, and describe the classroom and learning contexts for our program.

Through it all, the preparation and the instruction, remember to have fun. Fill your classroom with songs, poems, and games that teach spelling at a level children understand, and we believe that they, too, will come to see word study as inherently intriguing.

A Year-Long Approach to Spelling/Word Study

FOUR PHASES OF INSTRUCTION

Once we became aware that traditional spelling practices weren't working for many young children, we focused on what we perceived as weaknesses in those practices and researched, brainstormed, and tried out alternatives. These efforts ultimately resulted in the four-phase approach, encompassing a full school-year schedule of spelling/word study instruction, which we present in this book. Each phase builds upon previous phases and progresses into the next phase.

The subsequent chapters in the book are each devoted to a particular phase: Chapter 2—Phase One; Chapter 3—Phase Two; Chapter 4—Phase Three; and Chapter 5—Phase Four. The table below summarizes the flow of the phases and the major focuses of each phase.

A YEAR-LONG APPROACH TO SPELLING/WORD STUDY	
Approximate Time Line	*Focus*
Phase One (Sept–Oct)	Learning Sight Words: Visual and Auditory Sequencing Strategies
Phase Two (Nov–Dec)	Developing Phonological Skills: Rhyming and Phoneme Manipulation
Phase Three (Jan–March)	Building Words: Using Visual, Auditory, and Meaning Features of Known Words to Make New Words
Phase Four (April–June)	Making Connections: Using Common Word Families
Ongoing (Sept–June)	Integrating Effective Word Study Strategies

The progression through the phases can be summed up as follows: In successful spelling work, children continually build upon and expand their repertoire of known words by using their existing knowledge of sound sequences (phonemes), letter patterns (graphemes), and meaning units (morphemes) within words.

KEY ELEMENTS AND FEATURES

Following are the key elements and features of the approach:

⊙ Specific, essential spelling strategies taught via 5–10 minute mini-lessons and followed by opportunities for students to practice the strategies with decreasing levels of teacher support: teacher modeling, guided practice, independent practice, independent application. (See diagram on page 13.)

⊙ Independent practice activities in learning centers based on the needs of diverse learning styles, as described in Howard Gardner's book, *Frames of Mind: The Theory of Multiple Intelligences*, 1993.

⊙ Successful research-proven practices based upon the work of eminent researchers in the field of spelling/word study, including Richard Gentry, Patricia Cunningham, Fountas and Pinnell, and Marie Clay. Utilization of Richard Gentry's "Look-Say-Cover-Write-Check-Study" Strategy Sheet in lieu of the "writing spelling words 3x each" regimen.

⊙ Modification and adaptation of Reading Recovery word study practices, which were designed for individual intervention, so that they could be used with the whole class and with small groups.

⊙ The implementation of creative and authentic ways to awaken students' spelling consciousness and provide engaging opportunities for home support—for example, inviting students to search their homes for items to add to "Environmental Print 3-D Collages" (collages highlighting word families found in print on grocery items, books, signs, etc.: P**op**-tarts, p**op**corn, the book *H**op** on P**op***, st**op** sign) or, in place of the traditional homework practice of students' repeatedly writing spelling words in isolation, encouraging families to work at home together to author the "silliest rhyming sentence" for a class book.

⊙ An alternative set of assessments to replace the traditional weekly spelling test regimen, in which children would memorize a select number of focus words for a Friday test but would rarely transfer this new learning to their own writing pieces. The weekly spelling test did not appear to be improving students' mechanical writing performance; therefore, we decided to replace it with contextually-based dictations, such as the "Spelling Challenge." In this procedure we dictate 3–5 sentences, composed of high-frequency vocabulary words and words incorporating the essential phonograms, for the children to transcribe. We remind the students to edit their writing not only for correct spelling, but also for appropriate conventions of written language (e.g., proper spacing between words, capitalization, and punctuation rules). These weekly spelling assessments provide a much-needed opportunity for young writers to actually practice their newly learned editing skills. Prompted writing samples, along with students' own journal writing pieces, provide further valuable information that both teachers and students can use to jointly monitor spelling progress.

IMPORTANCE OF REVISITING WHAT'S BEEN LEARNED

The underpinnings of our spelling/word study program are continually revisited throughout this book. For example, syllabication is discussed in various chapters. However, in each phase the treatment is somewhat different from that in a previous phase. As children grow as spellers, their understanding of a skill or strategy grows: They begin to understand it at a new level. They learn to become more sophisticated listeners throughout the stages, and they become more aware of what they see in their environment. Our goal as teachers of spelling is first and foremost to teach our students, at their current level of understanding, a repertoire of spelling strategies to draw from when met with the challenge of spelling an unknown word.

Strategy-Oriented Approach vs. Skill-Oriented Approach to Spelling Practices

In the chart below, we summarize the major differences between our strategies approach and a more traditional, skills-based approach to spelling instruction.

SKILLS APPROACH VS. STRATEGIES APPROACH TO SPELLING PRACTICES	
Skill-Oriented Habituated Spelling Practices	*Strategy-Oriented Research-Based Spelling Practices*
Writing spelling words 3X/each	Utilizing Richard Gentry's "Look-Say-Cover-Write-Check" study strategy
Individually writing 10 words in complete sentences	Individually creating a single, illustrated "Silly Sentence" page for a class book
Alphabetizing lists of spelling words in isolation	Entering spelling words into personal dictionaries to utilize alphabetizing skills
Completing fill-in-the-blank worksheets	Creating classroom environmental print or 3D collages featuring spelling words or patterns
Taking weekly spelling tests of individual spelling words, dictated by the teacher and graded by the teacher	Among other instruction-related assessment measures, taking weekly spelling challenges of 3 to 5 sentences, composed of spelling words in context, dictated by the teacher and checked and self-corrected by students

Three Contexts for This Approach to Spelling/Word Study

This section presents an in-depth look at the research behind and classroom context for our recommendations about word study/spelling instruction. First, we look at what we consider to be two essential building blocks of knowledge for all good spellers. Then we switch to the classroom itself and examine both the components of the balanced literacy program and the model of gradual release of responsibility, or decreasing levels of teacher support.

NECESSARY BUILDING BLOCKS FOR GOOD SPELLERS

We believe that there are two things necessary to be a good speller of the English language: the ability to listen for the sequence of sounds within words, or *auditory sequencing*, and the ability to focus on the way words look, or *visual memory*.

Auditory Sequencing

We can enhance children's development of auditory sequencing by encouraging them to use "temporary/approximate" spelling. This allows them to freely express their thoughts in writing. Writers' Workshops (described in the next section) provide an established format for early primary-grade teachers to monitor their students' progression through developmentally-appropriate spelling stages. Within these contexts, children learn to more efficiently represent the individual sounds that they hear within words (Richard Gentry, 1993).

Auditory sequencing may also be developed through a variety of *phonemic awareness activities* that draw children's attention to syllables and then phonemes within words. Shared Reading of songs, poems, and rhyming books (described in the next section) provides children with an opportunity to grow comfortable with the sounds of our language. As students clap to the rhythm of familiar songs and rhymes, they are learning the essentials of syllabication.

Another way to approach auditory sequencing is by using the techniques of Russian psychologist D. Elkonin (1973). We include a number of these techniques—which involve the use of sound boxes—in our activities to facilitate students' awareness of sound sequences within words. They are also an essential, and very successful, component of Reading Recovery lessons, which we have used as a resource in developing our lessons.

Visual Memory

The second building block for a good speller, visual memory, must begin with young children's learning how to focus on and visually scan words. First they learn to note the length and shape of words, as well as the individual letter sequences; next, they learn how to re-visualize or memorize the spelling of a core of high-frequency words. In order to become successful spellers, children must be taught *how* to expand their core of known words by adding, deleting, and/or substituting letters within words (Patricia Cunningham, 1995).

WORDS OF NOTE

"With just 38 rimes students can write, spell or read over 600 relatively common one-syllable words."

—Edward Fry, *The Reading Teacher*, April 1998

BALANCED LITERACY PROGRAM

Based on a model by Fountas and Pinnell (1996), below is a brief description of each of the components of the balanced literacy program. You can teach all of our mini-lessons and guided practice activities within these components. By doing this, you can create a more authentic learning environment.

READ ALOUD/MODELED READING

The teacher shares a variety of literary genres with the children, modeling the joys of reading and encouraging the art of listening. During read-aloud sessions, the teacher has an opportunity to highlight particular passages that will guide students to understand the patterns and structures of written language (e.g., repetitive refrains, rhythmic patterns, and so on).

SHARED READING

The teacher invites children to listen and follow along in a book that she reads aloud. The book has enlarged print so the children can read along with the text. The teacher points out key word features and teaches word attack strategies. This is a perfect opportunity to teach the mini-lessons presented in this book.

GUIDED READING

Children with similar reading abilities are invited to work in small groups, using a leveled text that is at the group's instructional level. With support and explicit teaching, students learn and practice a selected reading strategy. Words focused on during word study are later highlighted during guided reading sessions. Students learn and practice spelling strategies.

INDEPENDENT READING

Children read independently or with partners and practice reading and spelling strategies that were taught during guided and shared reading. This is a great opportunity for children to apply reading and spelling strategies independently.

WRITE ALOUD/MODELED WRITING

Through a think-aloud process, the teacher demonstrates the steps in her own writing process including: brainstorming topic ideas, drafting, revising, and editing. The teacher again models and exposes children to a variety of literary genres and their unique language structures. Through explicit teaching in mini-lessons, the teacher focuses children's attention on particular aspects of word study.

SHARED AND INTERACTIVE WRITING

Students and teachers work together to compose a piece of writing, such as a morning message. Words from the class's current word study are included in this writing. This allows the teacher to draw attention to the critical word features that children are learning. The teacher may switch from a shared writing approach in which the children express their ideas and she acts as the scribe, to an interactive model in which she shares the pen and allows the children to join in the actual transcription process.

GUIDED WRITING

Children write a variety of texts as the teacher guides them in the actual application of newly taught spelling/word study strategies. During writing workshop sessions, the teacher conferences with students, monitoring and scaffolding their transcription skills, as the children *practice* essential spelling strategies.

INDEPENDENT WRITING

Children independently compose and transcribe their own pieces—anything from stories and poems to lists and letters. The teacher regularly assesses students' writing pieces as she evaluates their spelling progress. Students also have an opportunity to review their own work as they practice editing strategies.

GRADUAL RELEASE OF RESPONSIBILITY

The structure of our weekly spelling/word study program is based upon P. David Pearson's well-established and highly-regarded Gradual Release of Responsibility Model (Gallagher & Pearson, 1983). As you can see from the diagram on page 13, the three components of our weekly approach—mini-lessons, guided practice activities, and independent practice activities—are positioned along a continuum of decreasing levels of teacher support. This process, which involves explicitly teaching a spelling strategy in a brief (5–10 minute) mini-lesson and then directly following it up with guided practice of that strategy, encourages children to become involved in their own learning. Then, when they are ready to work independently, children are invited to practice what they've learned in an independent learning center. In this way, they begin to "own" the new strategies and need far less teacher support.

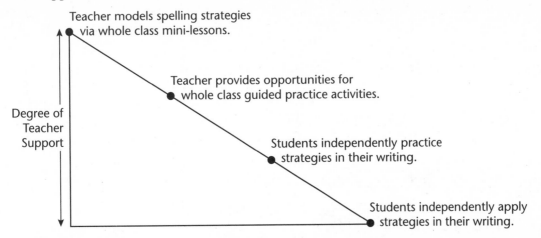

The Weekly Picture: Components of the Approach

The table below is a kind of weekly road map—a structure for organizing and planning each weekly word study workshop. Following the table, we offer further information on each of the major components.

With one exception, you'll find major sections in each chapter for each of the components listed in this table. That's because within each phase (and within each chapter in this book), we follow the same weekly routine and regular lessons, activities, and assessment pattern. The one exception is the material on Home Links, which you'll find in the Appendices (pages 118–123).

A WEEK IN WORD STUDY		
Day	**Workshop Component**	**What Happens**
Monday or Day 1	Model Mini-Lesson (5–10 minutes)	Teacher presents a brief strategy and skill lesson focusing on one principle of word study.
	Guided Practice (15–20 minutes)	Teacher demonstrates word study activity, models appropriate use of manipulatives, and invites children to practice learning strategy at their tables or desks.
Tuesday, Wednesday, Thursday or Days 2, 3, 4	Independent Practice: Classroom Extensions (40–50 minutes)	Children explore hands-on word study activities in differentiated learning centers. These activities are extensions of the guided practice demonstrations presented earlier in the word study workshop.
	Independent Practice: Home Link Extensions (10–15 minutes)	Children revisit and rehearse newly-learned spelling strategies, at home, via multi-sensory assignments.
Friday or Day 5	Independent Application: Assessment (30–45 minutes)	Teacher assesses spelling proficiency by evaluating journal entries, buddy check activities, and writing in context.

EXPLICIT TEACHING: MINI-LESSONS

All mini-lessons introduce a new spelling strategy and are taught to the entire class. We typically do this during a Shared Reading session, because Shared Reading offers a wonderful opportunity for children to see the features of words in a Big Book. You can hold these instructional sessions any time during the school day. The important thing is to make the lessons as real to the children's experience and environment as possible. If your class loves reading a certain type of book or genre, use it in your teaching. Using what your class already knows and loves will help you teach spelling most effectively. To help our young early readers, writers, and spellers stay on task, we have based our teacher prompts on the Reading Recovery Program's simple, repetitive prompts: "That's what good readers do," or "Does that make sense?" and so on. By carefully wording the comments in the lessons and activities, you can help your students more easily internalize key points or essential understandings.

GUIDED PRACTICE ACTIVITIES

The guided practice activities throughout this book can be taught in a whole- or small-group setting. You might choose to offer them immediately after your mini-lesson or, alternatively, on the following day. If you find that your children are excited to try something like clapping out syllables and want to practice right away, then by all means try to give them that chance. We must learn to read our children more and our plan books less. We want children to be able to play with words and notice patterns in language, visual and auditory. They can only do this if we give them regular opportunities to do so. When we teach them a spelling strategy, letting them practice it when interest is running high is probably the best plan of all.

INDEPENDENT PRACTICE ACTIVITIES

It is during independent practice activities that your children will be practicing on their own—and perhaps even teaching other students—the spelling strategies you have already taught during your mini-lessons and guided practice. Independent practice is a very important part of overall spelling/word study because it is here that students start to truly apply what they have learned. We have found it easiest to set up the independent practice as learning centers. A few simple learning centers targeted to skills and strategies you've been teaching in your spelling and reading program help to create an active learning process. The center space should be organized so that your children need only to concentrate on the spelling strategy. In the sections below, you'll find tips to facilitate your establishing and managing the independent learning centers.

> **Purposes for Using Independent Practice Centers**
>
> ⊙ Organizes all supplies needed for independent practice
>
> ⊙ Fosters a sense of independence for the learner
>
> ⊙ Frees up teacher time to work with small groups
>
> ⊙ Gives children a way to organize tasks to be completed in an allotted time
>
> ⊙ Rewards children for a job well done

Children learn through different modalities. What works beautifully for one child may be incomprehensible to another. If a child is encouraged to work at a center that is at cross-purposes with his or her learning modalities, frustration may build. With this in mind, we have set up our independent learning centers based on various learning styles. We also discuss this further below.

Managing Centers Where Real Learning Takes Place

⦿ Establish guidelines early in the year about how you expect children to be responsible for the supplies at each center (i.e., you expect caps to be placed on markers and placed back in the marker container). Be sure to praise the children when they follow proper procedure when cleaning up a center. Explain that orderly centers benefit everyone in the class community.

⦿ You might begin each Monday morning by going over proper procedures for the assigned activity at the learning centers. It pays off to take approximately 10–15 minutes to go over what needs to be completed at each center. When you introduce the activity based on a similar guided practice activity students have already completed, it is easier for children to pick it up.

⦿ Be patient. It takes a few weeks for children to get used to using centers and taking on responsibility. But in October when you look around the room and find all of your students engaged in an activity, knowing exactly what to do without your constant supervision, you'll probably feel as we always do—that this was really worth the effort!

⦿ Experiment with different techniques for running the centers, find the one that works for you and your students, and stick with it. You may find that what works one year with one group of children may not work another year. The most important part of teaching through learning centers is allowing children to become responsible for their own learning and thus fostering independence.

⦿ One way to help children become responsible for their own learning and to help you manage the centers more smoothly is to give students a weekly checklist at the start of the week. This checklist enumerates for children the centers they are responsible for completing that week. (See page 16.) Each day they choose what centers they want to visit that day. They have until Friday to complete the checklist. This technique is especially helpful for the student who finds it hard to organize and manage time. And most children seem to like choosing where they want to go that day. As they complete that task, they look around the room to find the next center that is available and go there (keeping in mind the magic number they have learned: no more than four at each center.)

⦿ There may be a student or two now and then who will check off a center and never actually visit that center. To avoid this, you might leave a space on the checklist for the name of the buddy a student worked with. A lot of the activities at the centers are games or involve partnerships. Having a student write down the name(s) of the children he or she worked with supports students who might be distractible.

⦿ Another method of managing centers is to assign groups of students to individual centers and allow an allotted amount of time at each center. At the end of the allotted period, the children move to the next assigned center. This gives you the flexibility to group children.

⦿ Whichever method you use, the beauty of the centers is the flexibility they provide: as some students move through individual centers, you meet with small groups for spelling instruction and/or guided reading.

⦿ You might find it helpful to play classical music during center time. This is a way for the children to monitor the noise level of the classroom. You can tell them, "If we can't hear the music, then we are being too loud." It is also fun to watch the children sway to Mozart as they are working.

Name _____

Have fun in centers this week!

_____ **1.** Play with shaving cream and spell words in the *in* family.

_____ **2.** Play "Go Fish" with a partner using your spelling words.

Name of person you played with: _____

_____ **3.** Play "Sight Word Puzzles."

_____ **4.** Make your spelling words in the pocket chart.

_____ **5.** Play "Beans in a Can."

Managing the Centers

A center space can be as simple as some desks moved together to form a table or, even more simply, an empty space in the corner of the room. Some centers lend themselves to being portable, while others—such as a reading area—should be perceived as permanent, dedicated spots throughout the year. Plastic containers with lids serve well as portable centers. All needed supplies can be easily stored inside the plastic container. Even when the location remains the same, the activities that take place within a particular center will change weekly or biweekly according to what you are teaching in word study. Using a center checklist such as the example above helps children know exactly which learning centers to complete. Gauge your students' progress; when they have mastered a strategy, change the activity within the center.

Multiple Intelligences

The independent practice activities are balanced to take into account the different learning styles that young children bring to the classroom. According to Howard Gardner's Theory of Multiple Intelligences, there are eight learning styles: Linguistic, Logical-Mathematical, Bodily-Kinesthetic, Spatial, Musical, Interpersonal, Intrapersonal, and Naturalistic. Each of these is described briefly in the chart on page 17.

WORDS OF NOTE

"The multiple intelligence theory posits that every child uses different combinations and degrees of each of the eight intelligences to learn about and respond to the world."

—Carlisle, 2001

GARDNER'S LEARNING STYLES	
Linguistic	These young learners enjoy literacy activities and writing.
Logical-Mathematical	These young learners are interested in patterns, categories, sequencing, and mathematical relationships.
Bodily-Kinesthetic	These young learners process information through bodily sensation and physical activity.
Spatial	These young learners process information through images and pictures.
Musical	These young learners are discriminating listeners who have a good sense of rhythm.
Interpersonal	These young learners have a highly-developed social consciousness.
Intrapersonal	These young learners are self-motivated and introspective in nature.
Naturalistic	This intelligence is not an obvious learning style in the area of word study.

HOME LINKS

Teachers know that to be truly successful with word study, children need practice and reinforcement at home. Parental involvement is key in any successful spelling program. For this reason, we include a Home Link section in our spelling program. At the start of each of the four phases, we recommend sending a letter home to parents explaining the upcoming goals of spelling and word-study instruction for that phase. We also recommend specific activities for Home Link use after certain lessons and activities. In the Appendices (pages 118–123), you'll find a model letter for each phase and an annotated list of the recommended lessons and activities.

TEACHER ASSESSMENT OF STUDENT LEARNING

In this approach, assessment is an informal, ongoing process. We emphasize "kid-watching," which is essentially a teacher's constant, non-intrusive observation of student learning behavior. We recommend that you record your observations regularly in an Observations Log. In addition, we have created and adapted several specific classroom-based assessment techniques for each phase. These instruments—such as contextual dictation or the student writing sample—are based on student classroom work and are thus directly connected to your instruction and to students' real learning. At the end of Chapters 2, 3, 4, and 5, you'll find assessment tools and strategies relevant to each particular phase.

Making Spelling/Word Study Kid-Friendly

Remember that word study is a child's exploration of words. Throughout this book, we have tried to come up with fun, authentic ways to incorporate words and spelling strategies into a primary child's world, but these are just a start for you in your own classroom. Use these activities and strategies either as they are or as models, and don't be afraid to come up with your own. After using this program in our own classrooms for a number of years, we have seen a dramatic change in reading ability, spelling ability, and writing ability. But what thrills us most of all is the change in our children's attitudes: They are excited about spelling and writing. One of the first steps in implementing successful word study and engaging children in an active learning process is to invite them to be facilitators of their own learning. Make your classroom a comfortable, kid-friendly space. Make it a place where children feel comfortable taking risks and are not afraid to experiment with language. Word study is a chance for early readers to explore words around them. When you set up your classroom, give children every opportunity to see words. Put print everywhere. Set up your classroom so that children have the opportunity to see the length and shape of everyday words. Your children will start to exercise their visual memory by reading the walls every day without knowing they are doing it. Here are some specific ideas:

- ◉ Chart poems you enjoy chanting with your class.

- ◉ Hang the words to songs you enjoy singing together.

- ◉ Make lists of words you are studying and place on word walls.

- ◉ Hang signs and labels on objects around the room so children know how to spell them (i.e. telephone).

- ◉ Hang a welcome sign on your door.

Think of it this way: as your students start to notice that the word *come* is inside the word *welcome*, your classroom becomes a place of discovery for early readers and spellers. These kinds of connections can be made daily if you set up your classroom as a hub of literacy. Over the years, we have observed the characteristics that make a good speller. And we firmly believe that all children can be good spellers if we just teach them the correct strategies.

Characteristics of Good Spellers

- ◉ They hear sounds and recognize patterns in language.
- ◉ They can manipulate these sounds to make words.
- ◉ They have a heightened auditory awareness of words.
- ◉ They have an auditory recognition of words.
- ◉ They have a heightened visual awareness of words.
- ◉ They have a visual recognition of words.
- ◉ They can use a known word to spell an unknown word. They develop a confidence to build on what they know.
- ◉ They can handle flexible strategies.
- ◉ They use word walls and varied resources in the room; they read the room.
- ◉ They can begin to edit their own work.
- ◉ They understand the importance of spelling. They write so that a reader can read their writing.

When children engage in an active learning process—like these first-grade boys playing sight word tic-tac-toe— word study becomes exciting.

18

Learning Sight Words: Visual and Auditory Sequencing Strategies

PHASE ONE: SEPTEMBER-OCTOBER

In our experience, the most rewarding part of teaching early elementary grades is watching and helping children become aware of the environmental print around them. No matter how often we witness this, it always brings fresh delight when a child starts to consciously notice the letters in common signs and logos (e.g., STOP, Burger King) and begins to "read the classroom walls." It is so exciting to hear a six-year-old lean over to her friend and ask, "How do you spell *it*?" "*It*? That's easy!" her friend replies, as she walks up to the chalkboard and points to the class weather chart. "See... 'It is cloudy today.'"

Smiles spread across our faces as we say to ourselves, "Yes! They are finally noticing."

This awakening does not happen by itself, and it does not happen as fluidly for all children as we would wish. So the important question for us as teachers is: How can we facilitate this print awareness for all of the children we teach?

The first step is essential: We need to create print-rich classrooms that capture our children's attention and provide for rich conversations about our written language. The walls of a dynamic literacy-oriented classroom are filled with student writing, poetry charts, Shared Writing messages, prominent labels (such as "Writing Center," "Homework Bin," or "Please do not touch our fish"). Big Books are propped open on easels for children to explore and classroom libraries are well-stocked with all kinds of books. In these ways, we fill our students' days with reading and writing activities that explore the key features of our written language.

Recognizing and memorizing essential sight words is the focus of our earliest spelling/word study mini-lessons because it awakens our young learners to the essential visual cueing system that all readers and writers must use. Our goal is to help our children understand the metacognitive strategies that successful spellers employ when mastering a core of high-frequency sight words. To help accomplish this, we use a pre-selected core group of 25 words as an integral part of Phase One. We assembled this core group from a list of 100 high-frequency words (Pinnell and Fountas, 1998) after informally assessing our students' early writing samples and reviewing the vocabulary demands of their guided reading books.

Following the outline of our approach presented in Chapter 1, this chapter provides brief mini-lessons, related guided practice opportunities, independent practice activities to enable students' application of newly-taught strategies, and contextually-based teacher assessment options for this phase.

Explicit Teaching: Modeling Strategies Through Mini-Lessons

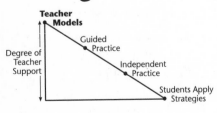

Through the following series of mini-lessons, we draw our students' attention to what good spellers do to learn sight words. A typical week of word study in this phase would launch with one of the mini-lessons outlined in the chart on the following page.

Overview of Model Mini-Lessons for Phase One

Mini-Lesson	Lesson Focusing Question	Lesson Purpose Statement
#1	What do good spellers do?	They use their eyes, ears, and mouth.
#2	What do good spellers look at in words?	They look at length, shape, and letters.
#3	What do good spellers listen for?	They listen for words in text, syllables in words, and sounds in words.
#4	How do good spellers begin to memorize sight words?	Short-Term Memory Strategy: They use their eyes to scan words from left to right. They notice regular and/or tricky letter patterns in words. Good spellers close their eyes and revisualize.
#5	How do good spellers study and internalize the spelling of common sight words?	Long-Term Memory Strategy: They look at the word, cover the word, and think about how the word looks. They say the word softly and write it from memory. A good speller then uncovers the word and checks to see if it's spelled correctly. If the word is spelled wrong, a good speller repeats this process.
#6	How do good spellers write sight words in context?	Good spellers write from memory. They ask themselves, 'Can I see the word in my mind?'
#7	How do good spellers edit their writing?	Good spellers use the word wall, personal dictionaries, and print around the room to check the spelling of common sight words.

Mini-Lesson #1

Essential Understanding: *"What do good spellers do?*

"They use their eyes, ears, and mouth."

Focus of Lesson: This mini-lesson focuses on heightening students' awareness of words, letters, and sounds that frequently appear in their reading and writing.

Whole-Class Instruction: Invite your students to listen, look for, and identify those familiar words—for instance, *the*, *up*, and *went*—that occur frequently as you read aloud a story from a Big Book, poem, or rhyme on an enlarged chart.

SAMPLE DIALOGUE:

Mrs. H.: Let's read and recite an old familiar rhyme together: "Hickory, Dickory, Dock."

(Teacher and children recite the rhyme as the teacher points to each word on an enlarged chart.)

Mrs. H.: Who can find the word *the* in this rhyme?

Lori: I can find the word *the* four times.

> **HICKORY, DICKORY, DOCK**
>
> Hickory, dickory, dock,
>
> The mouse went up the clock,
>
> The clock struck one.
>
> The mouse ran down.
>
> Hickory, dickory, dock.

Mrs. H.: Lori, please come up and use your magnifying glass to point to each *the* that you can find

(Mrs. H. repeats this direction, guiding students to locate other target sight words—up, went.)

Mini-Lesson #2

Essential Understanding: *"What do good spellers look at in words?"*

"They look at the length, shape, and letters."

Focus of Lesson: This mini-lesson models the strategy of focusing on the visual features of common sight words: length, shape, and letter sequence.

Whole-Class Instruction: Invite your students to take a closer look at several common sight words. The number of target words depends upon the ability levels of the students in your particular grade or class. We suggest that no more than three words be introduced at once.

SAMPLE DIALOGUE:

Mrs. H.: Let's look together at the word *said* and check its shape.

(Mrs. H. writes targeted sight word on the chalkboard, chart paper, or whiteboard.)
(Mrs. H. outlines the shape of the sight word.)

Mrs. H.: Is this a long word or a short word?

Lori: It is pretty short, like my name.

Mrs. H.: Yes, it is pretty short. How many letters are in this word?

SAID

Jason: Just four letters.

Mrs. H.: Let's check this word out from left to right and say the letters aloud as we read together.

Mrs. H. and students: *s-a-i-d*

Mrs. H.: Have you noticed this word in any of your reading books?

Lori: Yes, in our book *The Little Red Hen*. "The dog *said*, 'Not I.'"

(Lori points out the key word in her reading book.)

Mrs. H.: Great, Lori! That's what good spellers do. They remember where they have seen different words.

Model and repeat this strategy for two more words to ensure that children understand the process and can begin to apply it during the guided practice stage.

Spelling Success in the Early Grades • Scholastic Teaching Resources

Mini-Lesson #3

Essential Understanding: *"What do good spellers listen for?"*

"They listen for words in text, syllables in words, and sounds in words."

Focus of Lesson: This mini-lesson is actually made up of three separate but related mini-lessons, because children's phonological awareness skills need to progress through three stages. First, they gain an understanding that continuous talk or speech is made up of words. Next, they start to understand that words can be broken down into syllables. Finally, they begin to understand that words contain individual sounds, or phonemes.

Whole-Class Instruction, Part 1—Listening for Words: In the first of these mini-lessons, read aloud a popular traditional tale, such as "The Gingerbread Man," and ask students to identify which words and/or phrases the author keeps repeating (e.g., "Run, run, as fast as you can. You can't catch me. I'm the Gingerbread Man."). We recommend that you read additional poems, songs, and traditional tales during your daily read-aloud time to help students practice discriminating between words within texts.

Whole Class Instruction, Part 2—Listening for Syllables: The second mini-lesson addresses the strategy of listening for the syllables within words. Choose a familiar rhyme and place an enlarged version on an easel so everyone can see the text. As the class reads the rhyme chorally, invite the students to clap the rhythm. Then ask them to reread the rhyme. As they do, point to each syllable and invite children to continue clapping the rhythm. They will begin to notice and hear how some words are composed of more than one syllable.

SAMPLE DIALOGUE:

Mrs. H.: Let's recite the familiar rhyme "Twinkle, Twinkle Little Star" and clap the rhythm.

(Mrs. H. models how to clap to the syllables within words and then she draws wavy lines to underscore each syllable on the chart.)

Extension: You can integrate this lesson into other instruction several times throughout the day. Shared reading, interactive writing, and story time lend themselves to developing an ear for identifying syllables in words. Or you might draw the students' attention to specific words during a read aloud:

Mrs. H.: Boys and girls, let's stop for a moment. We just read a big word. Let's say it again: *hippopotamus.* Now let's clap it out. Hipp-o-pot-a-mus. How many syllables was that?

Julie: Five.

Whole-Class Instruction, Part 3—Listening for Sounds:
In this third mini-lesson, the teacher models for the children how we can hear and identify the individual sounds within words. To help students move beyond identifying syllables to hearing individual sounds in words, draw the following 2-, 3-, and 4-sound segment box models on a white magnetic board or chalkboard:

Model the sound segmentation task for the children by articulating several 2-, 3-, and

> Twinkle, Twinkle, little star
>
> How I wonder where you are,
>
> Up above the sky so high
>
> Like a diamond in the sky...

4-phoneme words: for example, me—2 phonemes, cat—3 phonemes, jump—4 phonemes. Do this slowly as you push magnetic counters into the boxes, sound by sound.

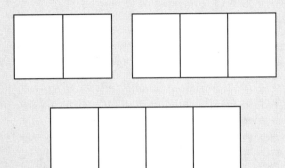

WORDS OF NOTE

"The goal of syllable training should be to increase awareness of the syllable structure of spoken words and the syllable types of English rather than to apply canned rules for visual segmentation of written words into syllable segments as defined by the dictionary."

—Virginia W. Berninger, et al, *Learning Disability Quarterly*, Spring 2000

SAMPLE DIALOGUE:

Mrs. H.: Today we are going to listen for the individual sounds that make up words. In order for us to hear each sound, we have to stretch the word and pronounce it very slowly...for example, *cat, c—a—t.* You say the word cat slowly with me.

Mrs. H. and students: *c—a—t*

Mrs. H.: Watch me push a counter into a box for each sound that I say in the word *cat.*

(Mrs. H. pronounces the word cat *slowly, c—a—t, and pushes one block at a time into each box.)*

Mrs. H.: How many sounds did we hear in the word *cat?*

Jason: Three.

Mrs. H.: Yes, Jason, there are three sounds in the word *cat.*

Repeat this activity several times to allow children to practice slowly articulating and identifying the sounds within 2-, 3-, and 4-phoneme words.

WORDS OF NOTE

Dr. Marie Clay reintroduced, as part of her successful Reading Recovery Early Intervention Program, a sound sequence analysis technique developed by Russian psychologist Elkonin. The use of sound boxes helps children hear and identify the sequence of sounds within words.

—Marie Clay, *A Guidebook for Teachers in Training*, 1993

TEACHER'S CORNER

For a fun variation, have children use rhythm instruments to beat out the rhythm of the words of the popular rhyme.

WORDS OF NOTE

"Phoneme segmentation is an excellent predictor of reading and spelling skill, even in the early stages of literacy development."

—Kate Nation and Charles Hulme, *Reading Research Quarterly, International Reading Association*, Vol. 32, 1997

Mini-Lesson #4

Essential Understanding: *"How do good spellers begin to memorize sight words?"*

"They use their eyes to scan words from left to right. They notice regular and/or tricky letter patterns in words. Good spellers close their eyes and revisualize."

Focus of Lesson: This mini-lesson extends students' attention to the visual features of print practiced in earlier mini-lessons—length, shape, and letter—and draws their attention to the critical or possibly challenging letter patterns in certain sight words, such as s*ai*d, w*a*s, and *by*.

Whole-Class Instruction: Write the targeted sight words on the chalkboard or whiteboard.

SAMPLE DIALOGUE:

Mrs. H.: Let's look at the word *said*. Let's check out this word from left to right and say the sounds aloud as we read together.

said   was

Mrs. H and students: *s—ai—d*

Mrs. H.: Were there any tricky parts where the letters and sounds were hard to match?

Brett: Yes, in the middle. It sounds like an /e/ sound, like in the word *red*.

Mrs. H.: Great, Brett, that's what good spellers do. They notice the tricky parts and try to remember the letter patterns.

Mrs. H.: Please close your eyes and try to see the letters in the word *said* in your mind. What letter comes first?

Lori: *s*

Mrs. H.: Next?

Andrew: *a*

Mrs. H.: Next?

Noah: *i*

Mrs. H.: And what letter comes at the end of the word *said*?

Whole class: *d*

Mrs. H.: Who would like to come up to the chalkboard and write the word *said* from memory?

In order to make this lesson truly effective, repeat it with another two or three sight words.

Mini-Lesson #5

Essential Understanding: *"How do good spellers study and internalize the spelling of common sight words?"*

"They look at the word, cover the word, and think about how the word looks. They say the word softly and write it from memory. A good speller then uncovers the word and checks to see if it's spelled correctly. If the word is spelled wrong, a good speller repeats this process."

Focus of Lesson: During this brief mini-lesson, demonstrate for the children how to effectively master new spelling words using J. Richard Gentry's "multimodal" study strategy: Look, Say, Copy; Cover and Write; Check (*Effective Practices for Spelling*, http://jrichardgentry.com, 2001). The goal of this method is to help sharpen visual memory.

Whole-Class Instruction: Ask the children to write the list of targeted sight words in the Word Study List column of the chart below.

Next, model for the children how to scan the word and say the sounds of the word (not the letters), as you copy the target word in the "Look, Say, Copy" column. Cover the word by folding the paper on the dotted line and rewrite the word (saying the sounds aloud), from memory, in the "Cover and Write" column. Lastly, fold back the paper and demonstrate for the children how you check the word for spelling accuracy. Explain that if the word is spelled correctly, they should place a check mark in the "Check" column of the page. If a word is spelled incorrectly, they should write it one more time in the "Check" column for reinforcement.

Home Link Connection: The students later use this Spelling Word Study Strategy Chart independently as a Home Link/home study activity. (See Appendix 1, pages 118–123.)

Name _____

Spelling Word Study Strategy

Word Study List	Look, Say, Copy (Study and then copy the word as you say it aloud.)	Cover and Write (Cover your word and try to write it all by yourself.)	Check (Check the word after you write it, and rewrite it, if you need extra practice.)
1. said	said	said	
2.			
3.			
4.			
5.			
6.			
7.			
8.			
9.			
10.			

Mini-Lesson #6

Essential Understanding: *"How do good spellers write sight words in context?"*

"Good spellers write from memory. They ask themselves, 'Can I see the word in my mind?'"

Focus of Lesson: During a Shared Writing Lesson, demonstrate the thinking process of proficient spellers. Model aloud how you use your "mind's eye" (J. Richard Gentry, Ph.D.) to visualize what a word looks like when you are required to write basic sight words.

Whole-Class Instruction: Invite children to jointly compose and transcribe a short morning message. (A morning message should always include several high-frequency vocabulary words.) A sample morning message is at right; the high-frequency words are shown in boldface type.

Stop each time before you write a common sight word (e.g., *on, to, the, see, for*) and model for the children what you do: you think back to when the class practiced studying that word and you "revisualize" what the word looks like.

> *October 2003*
>
> Good morning,
>
> Today our class will be going on a field trip **to the** pumpkin farm. We will **see** how pumpkins grow **in the** field. We will each pick one pumpkin **to** take back **to** class. Tomorrow we will decorate our pumpkins **for** our Halloween party.
>
> **By,**
>
> Ms. Moreno's Kindergartners

SAMPLE DIALOGUE:

Ms. M.: Boys and girls, today we are going to write our morning message together. I will demonstrate how good spellers stop to get a picture in their minds of how some words look.

(Ms. M. reads aloud the date and the greeting. She then begins to write the first sentence as she recites each word aloud. She stops when she reaches the word on.)

Ms. M.: *On* is one of our familiar sight words. I am thinking in my mind about what letters make up this word. Can you think in your minds along with me? Who can say the letters aloud?

Jason: *O—n* spells *on*. I remember seeing those letters on the light switch.

Ms. M.: Great spelling work, Jason.

(Ms. M. continues writing the rest of the morning message, stopping to demonstrate how to use one's mind's eye to spell the remaining targeted words: to, the, see, in, for, and by.)

Mini-Lesson #7

Essential Understanding: *"How do good spellers edit their writing?"*

"Good spellers use the classroom word wall, personal dictionaries, and print around the room to check the spelling of common sight words."

Focus of Lesson: This mini-lesson demonstrates for children that one way good writers edit their pieces is by checking for spelling errors or for words that do not look correct. The lesson helps students build a spelling consciousness and good spelling habits.

Whole-Class Instruction: During a Writer's Workshop session, invite students to check their own writing and circle three words on their drafts that "do not look right." Encourage children to use reference tools—the class word wall, personal dictionaries, and print around the room—to self-correct or verify the spelling of uncertain words.

SAMPLE DIALOGUE:

Mrs. H.: Boys and girls, today each of you will be reviewing one of your writing pieces with your editor's cap on. Remember, before our pieces are ready for publishing we must edit our work for grammar and spelling. Today we will focus on editing for spelling. Please look through your writer's notebooks and select one piece that you would like to edit today.

(After the children have selected their pieces, Mrs. H. distributes colored pencils or highlighters for them to use in the lesson.)

Mrs. H.: Please use your colored pencil to circle those words in your personal pieces that do not look right. What references could you use in the classroom to help you select your words?

Jason: We could use our word wall.

Whitney: We could also use our own dictionaries.

Lori: I found one of my words listed on our morning message chart.

Mrs. H.: What great word detectives you are! That's exactly what good writers do—they use print around the room, as well as references like dictionaries.

Guided Practice Activities

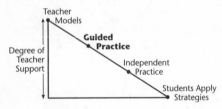

In this section, we offer 10 guided practice activities. Each activity accompanies a mini-lesson from the preceding section and helps students put into action what they have just learned in those lessons. These guided practice activities are interactive experiences that will enable children to "learn how to learn" common sight words; they can be used for whole-class or small-group lessons. The chart below provides an overview of the scope of these activities, their purpose, and the lessons they are intended to accompany.

Spelling Success in the Early Grades ● Scholastic Teaching Resources

Overview of Guided Practice Activities for Phase One

Guided Practice Activity	Use For	Accompanies This Mini-Lesson
Sky Writing	Visualizing words Letter formation	What do good spellers do?
I Spy, Hear, & Say	Visualizing words Listening for sounds Identifying words in context of print	
Word Detectives	Visualizing words Positioning of letters Sound/symbol relationship Visual scanning of words Identifying words in context of print	What do good spellers look at in words?
Word Sorts	Visualizing words Shape of words Sorting by visual features	
Listen for the "Beat": Clapping Names	Syllabication	What do good spellers listen for?
Sound Boxes	Identifying sequence of sounds within words	
Sight Word Clues	Visualizing words Visual features of words	How do good spellers begin to memorize sight words? (short-term memory strategy)
Look, Say, Cover, Write, Check	Transferring sight words to long-term memory	How do good spellers study and internalize the spelling of common sight words? (long-term memory strategy)
Fast Eyes	Visualizing words Automaticity of words	How do good spellers write sight words in context?
Using Classroom Materials (Reference Tools)	Visualizing words Using reference materials Self-correction	How do good spellers edit their writing?

Guided Practice Activity: SKY WRITING

Purpose: To practice writing sight words using correct letter formation and correct positioning of letters

Use for : Visualizing words; letter formation

Materials: Chart paper, easel, marker, storybook

Procedure: After modeling the correct spelling of a high-frequency word by writing it on chart paper, invite children to "write" the word in the air. Not only does this help students visualize and "see" the word, but modeling also helps the beginning writer with proper letter formation and handwriting skills.

SAMPLE DIALOGUE:

Mrs. M.: Today we'll be practicing the word *my Mmm-y*. Who can tell me what letter the word *mmm-y* starts with?

Patty: It starts with *m*.

Mrs. M.: Yes, Patty, it is the letter *m*. We write the *m* just like the letter *n* but...

Patty: With another camel's hump.

Mrs. M.: Yes. When we are writing an *m*, we start at the top, go down, back up and around, back up and around again. *Mmm-y*. Who thinks they know the next letter in *my*? It is just like the word *by* that we see on all the covers of our reading books before the author's name.

(Mrs. M. holds up a storybook and points to the cover.)

Sarah: It's *y*.

Mrs. M.: Yes, it's the letter *y*. The letter *y* goes down on a slant and then there is another slant that goes all the way down past the bottom line. Who would like to come up to the board and try writing the word *my*?

Allow time for a few children to come up to the easel and take turns practicing the correct letter formation and spelling of the word. After the children model this for one another, they are ready to try it on their own. Ask them to look at the word on the chart paper and then try "writing" it in the air while saying it aloud.

Guided Practice Activity: I SPY, HEAR, & SAY

Purpose: To identify in text sight words that have certain sounds

Use for: Visualizing words; listening for sounds; identifying words in context of print

Materials: Familiar songs, chants, or poems on chart paper; easel

Procedure: Write a poem or the lyrics to a familiar song on chart paper. Choose a word from the poem or lyrics and give clues about the word to students. As you'll see in the examples below, the clues can help you check each student's phonemic awareness ability.

SAMPLE DIALOGUE (to check blending):

Mrs. M.: I spy a word in "Twinkle, Twinkle, Little Star " whose sounds are /u/ /p/. What word has the sounds /u/ /p/? *(The teacher is articulating the sound of each letter, not the letter itself.)*

Frank: It's *up.*

SAMPLE DIALOGUE (to check phoneme segmentation skills):

Mrs. M.: I spy a word in "Twinkle, Twinkle, Little Star," and the word is *so.* Who can tell me the two sounds in the word *so?*

Dawn: /s/ /o/

SAMPLE DIALOGUE (to check phoneme deletion skills):

Mrs. M.: I spy a word in "Twinkle, Twinkle Little Star." The word is *star.* What is *star* without the /s/ sound?

Andrew: It's *tar.*

SAMPLE DIALOGUE (to check vowel substitution):

Mrs. M.: I spy a word in "Twinkle, Twinkle, Little Star." The word is *in.* What word would *in* become if I changed the letter *i* to an *o?*

Renata: It turns into *on.*

Extension: You can continue this game to check for children's ability to hear and identify sound deletions, substitutions, beginning and ending consonants, and so on.

Guided Practice Activity: WORD DETECTIVES

Purpose: To find sight words in the context of print

Use for: Visualizing words; positioning of letters; sound/symbol relationship; visual scanning of words; identifying words in context of print

Materials: Small magnifying glass (or one made from paper and laminate); Big Book for modeling; guided reading books for children

Procedure: Gather children for story time and read a familiar Big Book with them. After reading the story through, tell the children that you are going to read the story again, but this time you are going to stop every once in a while and try to find hidden sight words.

SAMPLE DIALOGUE:

Mrs. M.: I am told by the detective agency that the word *she* is hiding on this page. I need a detective to come up and use my magnifying glass and find the word *she.*

Sam: I can do that! *(He comes up to the Big Book and places the magnifying glass over the word.)*

(Mrs. M. repeats the process with other sight words throughout the book. The children then each get their own magnifying glass and a small guided reading book in order to find other sight words. After modeling the strategy in a large group, Mrs. M. might alternately take smaller groups of five children to practice it.)

Variation: You can also do this activity in a whole group, using a poem or familiar chant that you have written on chart paper. Laminate the poem and have the children come up and circle the hidden words with a marker.

Extension: Acting as a word detective and finding high-frequency words in poems, familiar chants and songs, and in books will also help to anchor a child when he or she reads. Anchoring is a very important way for beginning readers to make sure they are reading what is on the page. As the following example shows, discussing how a ship throws down its anchor provides a good analogy for explaining this:

SAMPLE DIALOGUE:

Mrs. M.: Has anyone ever seen a big ship?

Patricia: Yes, I went on a cruise. The boat was really big! It had an elevator and a pool.

Mrs. M.: Wow! Well let's say that ship wants to stop. How do they hold that ship in place?

Frank: With a big anchor.

Mrs. M.: Yes, that's right. They throw a big anchor over and that anchor digs in to the ocean floor and that ship stays in place. Well, we have anchors when we read, too. When you use your reading finger to point to the words while you read, your finger can act like an anchor.

Andrew: My finger is small. How can it do that?

Mrs. M.: Well, when your reading finger is going across all the words and you see a sight word that we've been practicing, such as *the*, *it*, or *to*, you know that you should throw out your anchor and think, "Is my mouth saying what my finger is pointing to?" If you're pointing to *the* but you're reading *sun*, then you know you're off track and need to go back to the beginning of the sentence and reread. Knowing all of those sight words will help you anchor yourself and check to see if you're in the right place while reading. Let's try this sentence together.

(Mrs. M. reads this sentence from the book: "I like the sun." She purposely tracks—or points— her finger incorrectly, and reads "I like sun.")

Children: No, you're wrong.

Mrs. M.: Uh-oh. My finger is pointing to the word *the*, and my mouth is saying *sun*. I am throwing my anchor out and saying this doesn't look right. I better go back to the beginning and try again.

Knowing words such as *the*, *it*, and *to* enables a child to track or follow his or her place during reading and therefore helps with fluency.

WORDS OF NOTE

"Fluency comes from the ability to immediately and automatically identify the most frequent words."
—Patricia Cunningham, 1995

Guided Practice Activity: WORD SORTS

Purpose: To sort words by common visual features

Use for: Visualizing words; shape of words; sorting by visual features

Materials: 10–15 index cards, with one sight word written on each card; erasable markers; pocket chart

Procedure: The purpose of a word sort is to focus children's attention on the various features of a word. Patricia Cunningham (1985) suggests that it is an effective method for increasing visual memory. When children begin to look closely at the features of words—at length, shape, the number of letters, initial sounds, final sounds, and endings—they begin to "see" what words look like. This enables them to make connections between words and to make connections from the known to the unknown ("*By* looks like the word *my* that I already know"). Word sorts help children to use these similarities to add to and build on their existing sight vocabularies.

To set up a word sort, first outline the shape of the word on each index word card. Then ask children to sort the cards for common characteristics. Depending on your students' needs and your particular lesson goals, you might tell the students which characteristics to look for in order to sort the cards. For example, you might tell them to select all words that end in the letter *s*. Other times you can tell the students to examine words such as *my*, *by*, and *day* and guess the common characteristic (the shape of the last letter, *y*).

> **TEACHER'S CORNER:**
> **Management Tip**
>
> To cut down on wear and tear, laminate word cards. Laminate some blank index cards, too, so you can add words to the pile using an erasable marker.

Guided Practice Activity: LISTEN FOR THE "BEAT": CLAPPING NAMES

Purpose: To identify the number of syllables within words

Use for: Syllabication

Materials: Chart of children's names (preferably in alphabetical order, so that you can easily discern how many children's names have the same beginning sound)

Procedure: Using the chart of your students' names, guide the class in clapping out the syllables in each name.

SAMPLE DIALOGUE:

Mrs. M.: Today we are going to explore the sounds of words and the syllables within a word. Does anyone know what a syllable is?

Miguel: It is a small part of a word.

Mrs. M.: Yes, Miguel. That's right—a syllable is a small part of a word. Let's clap out your name and discover how many parts, or syllables, are in it. I have a drum here and I will tap the drum for each syllable in your name: *Mi-guel*. How many taps did you hear?

Miguel: I heard two taps.

Mrs. M.: That's right. There are two taps or two syllables in your name. When I say taps, it means the same thing as syllables. Let's try someone else's name. How about Elizabeth? Listen for the syllables as I tap them out on the drum: *E-liz-a-beth*. How many taps did you hear?

Elizabeth: I heard four taps.

Mrs. M.: That's right! There are four syllables in Elizabeth's name.

Variation: Once the children are familiar with syllabication, have them move away from the comfort of using their names and begin this process with other words. An engaging game for doing this is "How Many Taps?" For this game, have available index cards with words the class is studying, as well as a chart divided into sections labeled "one tap," "two taps," "three taps," etc. Pick a word from the word box and invite the class to clap the syllables. Then have a child come up and place the word card in the proper section on the chart.

> ### WORDS OF NOTE
> *"At first, literacy learning is highly personal. There is no more important word to a child than his own name."*
> —Pinnell & Fountas, 1998

Extension: At every level of spelling development, children need to play with words. Because they love to discover the number of taps or syllables in their names, we have used this as a classroom management technique. We ask the children who have one syllable in their names to line up at the door, followed by two syllable names, and so on. There are many possibilities—for instance, we sometimes assign groups for cooperative learning according to the number of syllables in the children's names.

It's also fun to take large words you encounter daily and clap out the syllables in them. The children will start to make a connection between the size of a word and the number of syllables.

Guided Practice Activity: SOUND BOXES

Purpose: To focus on the individual sounds within a word

Use for: Identifying sequence of sounds within words

Materials: Sound boxes (see below for example); chips

Procedure: Choose a word (for example, *cat*) and write it with boxes drawn around each letter of the word.

While saying the word slowly, move a chip or marker to each sound within the word. A sound blend like /*sh*/ should be placed inside one box, because it's an individual sound made by those combined letters. This focuses children's attention on the individual sounds, allowing them to hear each one.

TEACHER'S CORNER: Management Tip
It is best to do this activity with no more than five children. You can also photocopy sheets with a varying number of blank boxes to have on hand. Depending on the word you choose for practice, pull out the sheet with the appropriate number of boxes, ask children to fill the word in, and you're ready for practice.

Sound boxes help young readers to slow down and discover the sound components of a word.

Variation: Have empty sound boxes on placemats and a container of chips. (See example above.) When you recite a word slowly, such as *c - a - t*, have children take chips and repeat the word slowly, pushing one chip in at a time.

TEACHER'S CORNER:
We have found that sound boxes work wonderfully with our struggling readers. It allows them an opportunity to slow down and dissect a word to discover its sound components.

Guided Practice Activity: SIGHT WORD CLUES

Purpose: To identify sight words based upon visual features

Use for: Visualizing words; visual features of words

Materials: Word wall

Procedure: One way to help children use visual features to identify sight words is with a game in which you choose a word, give clues, and ask children to use the word wall (see page 36) to figure out which word you chose. This game was suggested by Patricia Cunningham (1995).

SAMPLE DIALOGUE:

Mrs.M.: I am thinking of a word that has two letters. It begins with the /b/ sound. It rhymes with *my*.

Children: It's *by*.

Mrs. M.: I am thinking of a word that has 4 letters. It begins with the /f/ sound. You usually use it when you sign a note.

Children: It's *from*.

Mrs. M.: I am thinking of a word that starts with the /y/ sound. It has 3 letters and rhymes with the color of the sky.

Children: It's *you*!

TEACHER'S CORNER: Management Tip

Word walls provide an excellent opportunity to display the sight words that students have been working on. Word walls can be made in all different shapes and sizes to accommodate any size classroom. Use 26 pieces of oaktag, labeling each with a letter of the alphabet. Or divide a large piece of butcher block paper into 26 boxes. Teaching stores and catalogues also sell wonderful ready-made word walls, which consist of a large piece of felt, printed letter cards, printed sight word cards, blank cards to add your own words, and Velcro to attach the words to the word wall. If you make your own word wall, outline the shape of the sight word before attaching it to its proper spot on the wall to reinforce the shape of the word (as practiced in other guided practice activities). Laminate the cards to increase their utility. Whether you buy a pre-made word wall or make your own, be sure to put Velcro on all of the word cards. When the cards are prepared, alphabetize them and keep them in a file so you can easily pull the appropriate words for the week.

Aa
apple
ant

Oaktag

Aa	Bb	Cc	Dd
at	by		
Ee	Ff	Gg	Hh
			hello

Butcher block paper

Guided Practice Activity: LOOK, SAY, COVER, WRITE, CHECK

Purpose: To write words from memory

Use for: Transferring sight words to long-term memory

Materials: List of spelling words being studied; Look, Say, Cover, Write, Check reproducible (see page 52)

Procedure: Now that students have practiced a targeted number of words, it's time to transfer them to long-term memory. The "look, say, cover, write, check" technique can help with this.

SAMPLE DIALOGUE:

Mrs. M.: Today we're going to try to write the words we have been practicing from memory. I'm going to give everyone this piece of paper with four columns. In the first column, we are going to list the three words we have been studying this week. Let's write *the, see,* and *to* in that first column that says "Word Study List."

(Class does as instructed.)

Mrs. M.: Great. Now let's start with the word *the.* Look at it and copy it in the next column. Say the word *the* as you copy it. Then look at it, look at it, look at it, and keep looking at it until you can close your eyes and see it on your eyelids. Can you see it?

Chris: No.

Mrs. M.: Then open your eyes and keep looking at it.

Alessondra: I can see it.

Mrs. M.: Great. How's everyone else doing? Can you see it yet? When you can see it, fold the paper on the dotted line and cover the word. Try to write *the* in the "Write" column.

(The children write the word the *while the word is covered.)*

Mrs. M.: Now let's unfold and check your work. If you're correct, put a check mark in the "Check" column. If you're incorrect, repeat the steps and try again.

(The children continue this procedure with the remaining list of words.)

Guided Practice Activity: FAST EYES

Purpose: To automatically identify sight words and write them

Use for: Visualizing words; automaticity of words

Materials: Overhead projector; overhead transparency; erasable marker; list of sight words being studied; paper and pencils for students

Procedure: Using an overhead projector, a transparency, and an erasable marker, write one of the sight words being studied on the transparency while the overhead projector is off. Then direct children's attention to the screen and ask them to watch for the word. Next turn the light on for one quick second and turn it off quickly saying, "Fast Eyes." This game demonstrates how quickly the brain can recall a word, and it's one of our students' favorites. Children find it extremely entertaining—they're amazed at how fast the brain registers a word.

SAMPLE DIALOGUE:

Mrs. M.: We've been practicing lots of sight words. Let's take a look at the word wall and see how many we already know.

Dawn: I see 10.

Mrs. M.: Let's read them together.

(Mrs. M. points to the words on the word wall and they read the words together.)

Mrs. M.: Today we're going to play a game called "Fast Eyes." We're going to find out just how fast your eyes can recognize these words from the word wall. I'm going to pick one word and write it down on my overhead paper. *(She writes a word.)* Okay. I'm done. Now take a look up at the screen. You're going to watch for the word and when you see it, write it down on your paper. *(She flicks the switch on and off.)* Now write what you saw. What was it?

Class: It was *the.*

Mrs. M.: Now I'm going to turn the light back on. Check your work.

WORDS OF NOTE

"As soon as possible, children should learn to read and write these words for two reasons. When children at an early age learn to recognize and automatically spell the most frequently occurring words, all their attention is freed for decoding and spelling less frequent words and, more important, for processing meaning. The second reason we do not want children to decode or invent-spell these words is that many of the most frequent words are not pronounced or spelled in predictable ways."

—Patricia Cunningham (1995)

Guided Practice Activity:
USING CLASSROOM MATERIALS (REFERENCE TOOLS)

Purpose: To use classroom materials as a reference to self-check spelling

Use for: Visualizing words; using reference materials; self-correction

Materials: Classroom library; posters; charts; labeled items in your classroom (clock, door, etc.); word wall

Procedure: In order for children to become independent word detectives—finding, reading, and spelling words on their own—they must be surrounded by a reading-friendly, print-rich environment. There is a great deal you can do to create such an environment in your classroom, from labeling familiar items in the room to setting up an inviting classroom library. Point out all of the print that is available, and frequently encourage students to look around the room and use the many resources they find.

Below we list a number of ideas to help you develop a literacy-friendly classroom. Once you have provided your students with such access to high-frequency words through everyday, ordinary means, model for them how to find and use these means, and then allow many opportunities to explore. This is the ultimate goal: helping children to develop into independent word detectives always on the look-out for words to learn.

Ideas for Making Print Easily Accessible in Your Classroom:

⊚ Label all items in the classroom (clock, desk, door, etc.).

⊚ Hang posters with poems containing high-frequency words.

⊚ Hang familiar chants and songs on posters.

⊚ Position your word wall in a place where children can see it clearly and, if possible, where they can touch it.

⊚ Be certain your guided reading books and classroom library books are available for children to peruse at their leisure.

Ideas for Sparking Children's Interest in Books:

⊚ Make your classroom library inviting by providing child-sized chairs, pillows, benches, or even a couch. You might also add stuffed storybook characters such as Clifford, the Cat in the Hat, or Arthur to create a warm and cozy environment.

⊚ Institute a check-out system with library cards in the back of each book so children can borrow books overnight. Designate one child each week to hold the position of class librarian. Put that child in charge of collecting the signed out cards.

⊚ Remember, when reading is viewed as fun, children will be drawn to this special place in your classroom.

TEACHER'S CORNER:

One very active boy in our class had been spoken to several times for socializing. When he got up a fourth time, we jumped to the conclusion that he was on his way to his friend's desk once again. Only this time, he stopped at the bookshelf and started scouring through all of the guided reading books. When asked what he was doing, he replied, "I want to write the word *to* and I remembered it was in the title of the book we read yesterday." He started beaming from ear to ear when he heard these next words: "Michael, that is exactly what good writers do. Way to go! Good remembering!"

Independent Practice: Learning Center Activities

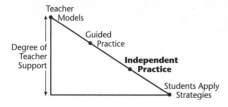

After mini-lessons and guided practice, we provide students with an opportunity to explore a range of hands-on activities that reinforce their study of sight words and the interaction of the various word study strategies. The following learning center activities offer young children independent practice of word study strategies. As the diagram above shows, these activities are far along the spectrum of decreasing levels of teacher support. Each activity includes a period of modeling and instruction—essentially, an introduction to the activity. After this introduction, place the activity in a learning center and make it available to the class. It is here that the independent learning takes place. The activities presented here are balanced to take into account the different learning styles that young children bring to the classroom. As we noted in Chapter 1, Howard Gardner's Theory of Multiple Intelligences establishes eight learning styles: Linguistic, Logical-Mathematical, Bodily-Kinesthetic, Spatial, Musical, Interpersonal, Intrapersonal, and Naturalistic. Each independent practice activity we present here is linked to one or more of the multiple intelligences.

WORDS OF NOTE

"The multiple intelligence theory posits that every child uses different combinations and degrees of each of the eight intelligences to learn about and respond to the world"

—Carlisle, 2001

Overview of Independent Practice Activities for Phase One

Independent Practice Activity	Learning Style Connection	Purpose
Fun with Magnetic Letters	Bodily-Kinesthetic and Spatial	Reinforce visual memory of sight words
Writing Words in Shaving Cream	Bodily-Kinesthetic and Spatial	Reinforce visual memory of sight words
Go Fish Game	Linguistic and Interpersonal	Reinforce visual memory of sight words and practice cooperative social skills
Sight Word Puzzles	Linguistic and Spatial	Reinforce visual memory of sight words
Beans in a Can	Musical	Reinforce auditory recognition of sight words and listen for individual sight words
Sound Boxes	Musical	Identify individual letter sounds in sight words and reinforce auditory discrimination of sounds

Independent Practice Activity: FUN WITH MAGNETIC LETTERS

Learning Style: Spatial and Bodily–Kinesthetic Intelligences

Purpose: To reinforce the visual memory of sight words by manipulating letters and arranging them spatially in the correct order. Sign language finger-spelling is another form of this kinesthetic and visual sequencing of letters to make words.

Materials: Magnetic letter set (lower case letters); magnetic white board or chalkboards (large size for teacher demonstration lesson and small student sizes for guided and individual practice); cookie trays; sign language alphabet letter charts. (See page 42 for a reproducible sign language alphabet chart that you can use to make large class-size and individual student charts.)

Modeling and Introduction: Prior to modeling this activity, place only lower case letters on the white board in alphabetical order. The sight words are *the*, *is* and *by*.

SAMPLE DIALOGUE:

Ms. K.: Today we're going to use the magnetic letters to build the three new sight words we learned this week. What do you notice about these letters?

Leah: They are all small-size letters.

Jose: They are like in the ABCs—*a* comes first and then *b*. (*He starts to recite the alphabet.*)

Ms. K.: Who can build our first sight word, *the*, using the magnetic letters?

(*Leah comes to the board and picks out the letters to build* the.)

Greg: It's easy to find the letters when you know that *h* and *e* are at the beginning of the alphabet and *t* is more at the end.

Ms. K.: Let's all say the as Leah slides her finger under the letters on the board. Let's try to finger-spell the word using our sign language alphabet chart. (*The children finger-spell the word* the.)

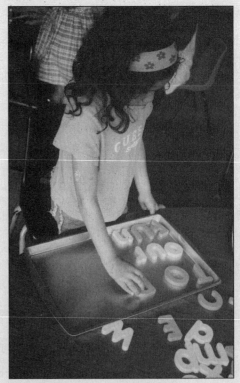

Magnetic letter activities reinforce visual memory of sight words.

(*Ms. K. asks Leah to scramble the magnetic letters for* the *and to invite another student to come up and put the letters in the correct order again.*)

To reinforce learning, it is important to repeat this activity. For each of the two other sight words—*is* and *by*—have students work in pairs using individual white boards (one for each pair), slates, or cookie trays. As you circulate, have one child in each pair build the word and then finger-spell it using the individual sign language alphabet chart. The partner scrambles the letters, finger-spells it in the correct order, and the first child rebuilds the word again. Have children practice this activity with each sight word.

Learning Center Activity: Once students have mastered the process of building and rebuilding sight words using the magnetic letters, this activity can be used as one of the centers for reinforcing sight words during the word study time. Also, once you have modeled and introduced the next hands-on activities (shaving cream and variations, below and on page 43), have students rotate through several different manipulative activities as centers during the word study period.

Extension: Using a sign language alphabet sheet, have one child in each pair finger-spell a word while the partner child says the word and builds it with the magnetic letters. Children can also work in pairs to try other known words found around the room on objects you have labeled, such as a door or a desk.

TEACHER'S CORNER

It is very important to include a sharing time at the end of each independent activity period so that children can describe their learning and experiences to their peers.

Independent Practice Activity: WRITING WORDS IN SHAVING CREAM

Learning Style: Spatial and Bodily-Kinesthetic Intelligences

Purpose: To reinforce memory of the sight words and the order of the letters using the kinesthetic (physical/tactile) experience of forming the letters of each word in shaving cream. This activity also reinforces correct lower case letter formation.

Materials: Shaving cream (any brand) in containers; small slate board or clipboard; flat specified area such as a desk or table.

Modeling and Introduction: Ms. K. invites students to watch carefully as she uses a small slate board to demonstrate this activity.

SAMPLE DIALOGUE:

Ms. K.: Today we are going to use shaving cream to write the three sight words we learned yesterday.

Greg: Shaving cream—wow! That sounds like fun! How can you write with shaving cream?

(Ms. K. writes her initials in shaving cream on the slate board. She asks students to notice how she uses only one hand—the hand that holds a pencil—to make a small shaving cream pond.)

Ms. K.: Notice how I use just my pointer finger to make letters and then I use the flat part of my hand to erase that letter. If I get too much shaving cream on my hand, I just wipe it off on the edge of the board.

Tanya: Can I try to write my name?

(Ms. K. invites Tanya to use the pond of shaving cream to demonstrate writing each letter of her name and erasing it.)

(At this point, Ms. K. discusses with the children some of the appropriate rules for using shaving cream, such as only working with their own pond and not getting the shaving cream on clothes or in eyes. She then asks the children to sit at their tables or desks, putting just their writing hand on the desk. She walks around and forms the initials or first name of each student, and finally has all of the children make their own ponds and practice writing and erasing their names.)

Finger-Spelling Alphabet

A	B	C	D
E	F	G	H
I	J	K	L
M	N	O	P
Q	R	S	T
U	V	W	X
	Y	Z	

Spelling Success in the Early Grades • Scholastic Teaching Resources

Ms. K.: Let's see if we can remember the letters in the first sight word we learned this week. Write the word *no* and check it with your neighbor to see if his or her letters match yours. I will touch you lightly on the head and then you can erase your word and write it five more times, erasing the word each time and saying it as you write it.

(Ms. K. repeats this process with the other two sight words, providing individual help with the correct sequence of letters and letter formation. When she gives the appropriate signal for clean up, students wash their hands and clean up their area with a wet and dry paper towel.)

Learning Center Activity: Once children have completed this activity as a whole group and have become familiar with the procedures, they are ready to practice it as an independent activity in their word study centers.

Extension: As children finish writing their sight words, invite them to practice other words in the room or on the word wall. Have them ask the student at the next desk or table to name the word they wrote.

Variations: In lieu of or in addition to shaving cream, you can use finger paint, instant pudding, or fun foam paint for this activity. If you use instant pudding (already mixed) or finger paint, it's best to provide individual finger painting paper for each student.

> **TEACHER'S CORNER**
> When you use this activity at word study centers, make sure that cleaning supplies—such as wipes, wet paper towels, or sponges—are available at the centers.

Independent Practice Activity: GO FISH GAME

Learning Style: Linguistic and Interpersonal Intelligences

Purpose: To reinforce visual memory of sight words and to practice cooperative social skills

Materials: Two to four (duplicate) sets of laminated index cards with spelling sight words written on them

Modeling and Introduction: Demonstrate the game to the whole class as they sit in a circle. Choose two children to come to the front of the room and deal six cards to both. Put the rest of the cards in a stack in the center between the players. Ask each player to check his or her set of six cards and place any matches in a single pile. The goal is for each player to match his or her remaining cards. At each child's turn, have him or her ask the other player for the desired card. If the other player has it, he or she must give it to the first child. If not, then the original player has to "go fish" and draw one card from the stack of cards in the center. The player who matches all of his or her cards first wins.

> **TEACHER'S CORNER**
> It is helpful to leave blank index cards and markers at the learning center so that new words can be added to the game.

Learning Center Activity: Once the game has been demonstrated and understood, the children can play in pairs at the center. (There should be no more than four children at a center for this activity.)

Independent Practice Activity: SIGHT WORD PUZZLES

Learning Style: Linguistic and Spatial Intelligences

Purpose: To reinforce visual memory of sight words; to organize letter puzzle pieces to match up and make a recognizable word

Materials and Preparation: Markers; plastic bags for storage; colored card stock paper for a teacher-made game. Make the game by writing the weekly mini-lesson's sight words on individual strips of card stock or on an $8\frac{1}{2}$" by 11" sheet. Laminate the words and cut them apart so that each puzzle piece has only one letter of the sight word. Store the puzzle parts for each sight word in individual small plastic bags. In the beginning of the year, we recommend that you put only the letters for one sight word in a particular bag. Later on in the year, the plastic bags can contain several cut-up sight words for increased challenge.

Modeling and Introduction: Gather the class into a circle and model the activity for the whole group. Take the puzzle pieces out of the bag and ask a student to put together one of the sight words presented in that week's mini-lesson. When the student has put the pieces together, invite him or her to call on another child to say the word. Then have children carefully return the pieces to the bag and repeat the process with a different bag.

Learning Center Activity: Have children work in independent learning groups of 5 or 6, taking turns putting the puzzle pieces together to form sight words and then checking them on the class word wall.

Extension Activity: Extend this activity by having the children themselves create the puzzle pieces. Provide strips of card stock paper, markers, and scissors at a learning center so that children at this center can write sight words on the strips and cut them apart for others to put together.

TEACHER'S CORNER
Some school supply stores and catalogues sell ready-made blank puzzles with 4, 8, or 12 pieces, which you can use to make word puzzles.

Independent Practice Activity: BEANS IN A CAN

Learning Style: Musical Intelligence

Purpose: To reinforce the auditory recognition of sight words and to listen for individual sight words in songs and poems

Materials: Coffee cans and beans; the songs "The More We Get Together" and "Bingo" (or other familiar rhymes and songs) written on chart paper and on individual student copies

Modeling and Introduction: Invite children to join you in a circle on the rug. Ask one student to point to the words of a song displayed on a chart at the front of the room while everyone else repeats the words aloud. Make sure that two or three words in the song are highlighted—for example, *we* and *get* in the song "The More We Get Together." As the children sing or say the words of the song, have them drop a bean in their cans each time they hear the first designated word. At the end of the song, ask them to check the number of beans in their cans against the chart to make sure that it matches the number of times they heard the word. Have the class repeat the process with the next designated word. The game continues as individual children come forward, point to a word, and ask classmates to drop a bean in their cans every time they hear the designated word in the song. Students may also share a can or container for the beans with a partner. Each set of students should have 6–7 beans to use.

Learning Center Activity: Once the game has been demonstrated and understood, have children play in independent groups at the center.

It is helpful to have an adult facilitator—for example, a parent volunteer—to assist students with this activity until they have mastered the procedure and are working together cooperatively.

Variations: The activity can be varied as follows: While an individual (teacher or student) reads the song or poem aloud and drops a bean in a can, other students find and circle the word on a photocopied sheet of the poem or song. Later they match the number of words they circled to the number of beans in the pot. Alternately, they might place the beans on top of the word on the photocopied sheet.

Another variation on this activity is to use a cassette tape of the song or poem. With earphones, the children listen to the tape and drop a bean in their can as they hear a specific word. The group checks with each other at the end of the tape to see if the beans in their cans match the number of times they heard the words.

> **TEACHER'S CORNER**
> Musical children are often singing to themselves or drumming on something. They are usually quite aware of the sounds others miss. These children tend to be highly discriminating listeners.

Independent Practice Activity: SOUND BOXES

Learning Style: Musical Intelligence

Purpose: To identify individual letter sounds in sight words and to reinforce auditory discrimination of sounds in sight words

Materials and Preparation: Small-size wood blocks or colored chips (two, three or four per student) and at least six oaktag cards per group. To create the oaktag cards, draw lines to divide the paper into two, three, or four equal parts and write sight words (putting one letter in each box) within the lines. (See the sample card on page 34.)

Modeling and Introduction: Model this activity for the whole class by saying a word normally and then by saying it very slowly. Explain to the children when you say it slowly, you are '*stretching out the sounds like pulling a piece of bubble gum out of your mouth.*' Then have the class repeat the activity. Ask them, "How many sounds do you hear in the word *m-a-t*?" The children hold up fingers to indicate the number of sounds they heard. Next show the group a card with a sight word written on it and boxes drawn around each letter. Invite one student to come to the front of the class and move a small block or chip into each appropriate sound box on the card as the class says the word slowly. The children may need to practice pushing the blocks or chips into the boxes several times before they are ready to move to the independent learning center.

Independent Learning Center This center works best with four to six students. It should be set up with at least three to four blocks or colored chips per student and a set of six to eight word cards. In the beginning of the year the children will work with only two or three blocks at a time, but as the year progresses, you can include cards with as many as four boxes for longer words such as *said* or *went*.

The activity works this way: The word cards are placed in a pile on the table. Each child has a partner. One student says the word on the card normally and then repeats it slowly as the partner pushes the blocks or colored chips onto the letters of the sound he or she hears. It is helpful to have a parent volunteer checking to see that the children connect the letter sounds to the number of blocks. The parent volunteer can also help children handle surprise discoveries that may occur—for instance, children will notice that some of the letters in the sight words do not make a sound and are 'silent.'

After the students have become familiar with this Elkonin activity, they can take turns saying a word from the word wall (without using the word cards). After saying it normally, the child repeats the word slowly as the others in the group push forward a block or chip for each sound or phoneme they hear in the word.

Extension: Students in this center can sort out and put into category piles the sight word cards according to the number of sounds they heard in each word.

TEACHER'S CORNER

This activity is essential for children who have difficulty sequencing sounds in words.

Teacher Assessment of Student Learning

We have found that informal observation and classroom-based, specific assessments are the most effective measures for ascertaining what children know and what they still need to learn. After children have had multiple opportunities to practice strategies for learning sight words in both reading and writing contexts, it is time to assess whether the target words have become part of their repertoire.

WORDS OF NOTE

"Teachers who develop useful assessments, provide corrective instruction, and give students second chances to demonstrate success can improve their instruction and help students learn."

—Thomas R. Guskey, *Educational Leadership*, February 2003

ONGOING ASSESSMENT

In order to attain this goal, "kid watching" (a term introduced by Yetta Goodman, 1978) is essential. Informal observations collected throughout the day—during writing centers, interactive writing, reading response journals, and Writers' Workshop—shed light on what strategies students are still developing and those that they are applying independently.

Observations Log

We recommend using an observations log formatted like the one below to record your observations. In a log like this, your priority is to highlight the behaviors and attitudes young writers bring to paper.

Child's Name	Date	Observations

MANAGEMENT OF LOG

- ⊙ Record observations for no more than four children per day. This will allow you to focus on these selected children, while remaining accessible to the rest of the class.

- ⊙ Punch holes in the log to store in a three-ring binder or clip to a clipboard.

OBSERVATIONS MADE ON LOG

- ⊙ The focus of your observations should be on the child's use of sight words. Questions to keep in mind include:

- ⊙ Is the child writing the sight words from memory?

- ⊙ Is the child using reference tools (classroom word walls, personal dictionaries, and/or print around the room) to help him/her with the writing?

- ⊙ Is the child sounding out sight words?

The most valuable way to use your observations log is to drive instruction. It's important to take some dedicated time to review the writing behaviors observed. The goal is to discern patterns of strengths and weaknesses in order to choose future mini-lessons.

Let's take a look at Mrs. Varrone's first-grade class during the month of September. Mrs. Varrone visited one table of four children. She recorded each child's name, the date, and specific strategies (or lack of) that she noticed.

Child's Name	Date	Observations
Tracey	9/20	Sight words were automatic Checking word wall
Debbie	9/20	Sounded out sight words Spelling sight words incorrectly
Gina	9/20	Spelled the and to correctly
Eileen	9/20	Used some inventive spelling

After reviewing the log, Mrs. Varrone noticed that three out of the four children had not checked their work. Now she knows that the focus of her next mini-lesson will highlight the importance of using reference tools in the classroom.

SPECIFIC CLASSROOM-BASED ASSESSMENTS

In addition to informal observations, be sure to allot time to more formally evaluate individual students' acquisition and application of the targeted sight words. The five specific classroom-based assessment tools listed below can provide these valuable, more formal insights about learning. (Note that in the discussions following this list, we provide detailed information on the latter three items. Administration of the first two—having students read and spell sight words in isolation—is already a familiar process to most classroom teachers.)

- ◉ **Sight Word Reading List:** Teacher asks student to read the list of required (25) high-frequency words. (See Appendix 3, page 126, to select 25 words from the "One Hundred High-Frequency Words.")

- ◉ **Sight Word Spelling**: Teacher dictates individual high-frequency words from target list.

- ◉ **Spelling Challenge Dictation Assessment** (contextually based assessment): Teacher dictates 3–5 sentences incorporating target sight words.

- ◉ **Cloze Assessment** (contextually based assessment): Teacher distributes individual cloze format assessment sheets.

- ◉ **Student Writing Sample:** Teacher selects a writing sample from student's journal to review and assess the student's application of Phase One strategies.

After gathering feedback from the above measures, you can use the Student Spelling Evaluation Checklist (see page 50) to record it.

Spelling Challenge Dictation Assessment

Spelling Challenges are dictation tests that take place at the end of weekly word study. In these tests, dictate sentences containing words from a target word list to children. The children begin to understand the importance of writing for meaning when the words are featured in context. This fosters reading and writing comprehension, and provides the children a review of previous spelling words.

The Spelling Challenge can be used to assess a child's expanding sight word and word family vocabulary. Make up sentences that contain many weekly target words, unique to grade level and classroom needs, and dictate them to children. Tell the students to listen to each target word in context to establish meaning. After reading the whole sentence, break it down a word at a time to make the task more manageable for early writers. The children practice writing sentences with appropriate capitalization and punctuation. The following dialogue illustrates the "Spelling Challenge" process.

SAMPLE DIALOGUE:

Teacher: Okay, boys and girls. Are you ready for a spelling challenge?

Children: Yes!

Teacher: Please listen carefully as I read the first sentence. I'll repeat it slowly when it's time for you to write. Number one: "I like going to the zoo."

(Children begin to write.)

Teacher: *(Reads slowly)* I...like...going...to...the...zoo.

Teacher: Before I read number two, let's edit our work. What do we need at the beginning of a sentence?

Children: We need a capital letter.

Teacher: That's right! Please check to make sure you've started your sentence with a capital letter.

Teacher: What do we need at the end to show it's a telling sentence?

Children: We need a period.

Teacher: What great writers you are! Please make sure you've ended your telling sentence with a period. Now we're ready for sentence number two. Please remember to listen carefully before you begin writing.

Have children write these sentences in a "Spelling Challenge" notebook. Send the notebook home every Friday so that parents can see and support spelling progress. The children are responsible for correcting any mistakes made during the Spelling Challenge, including those related to capitalization and punctuation. This process reinforces word study, appropriate conventions of print, handwriting skills, and the editing process.

Cloze Assessment: "Morning Message Format"

The morning message—a brief, daily, prominently-posted note to the students—is not only a warm way to greet young learners in primary classrooms, it provides a wonderful opportunity for shared reading and writing throughout the year. It can be used to support effective reading and writing strategies while building community in the classroom. As children acquire and build upon a basic store of sight word vocabulary, the morning message can be used as an assessment tool in cloze format.

The cloze works as follows. On a daily basis, provide the children with a list of the weekly sight words that have been highlighted in that day's morning message. At the end of weekly word study, distribute a copy of one day's message, substituting blanks for target sight words. After reading the morning message (chorally with younger children), instruct them to fill in the blanks one sentence at a time. (See below for a sample.) Depending upon students' spelling level and/or proficiency, appropriately adapt and/or modify this sample.

SAMPLE DIALOGUE:

Teacher: Let's read our morning message from Monday! Please read it with me as I point to the words.

(Teacher and children read message aloud.)

Teacher: Great job! Listen to the first sentence. "Today is Monday."

(Teacher pauses for a moment.)

Teacher: What is the first missing word on our sheet?

Children: *is*

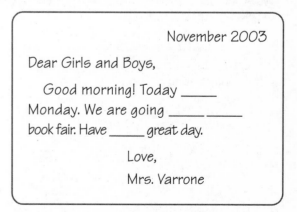

November 2003

Dear Girls and Boys,

Good morning! Today _____ Monday. We are going _____ _____ book fair. Have _____ great day.

Love,

Mrs. Varrone

Teacher: That's right. Please write the word *is* on the first line.

Teacher: Listen to the second sentence: "We are going to the book fair." There are two words missing in this sentence. Can you fill them in as I dictate the sentence to you?

Children: Yes.

    Teacher: We…are…going…to…the…book…fair. *(Children fill in the blanks.)*

    Teacher: Last sentence, here we go! "Have a great day!" What is missing in the last sentence?

Children: *a*

    Teacher: You are listening very carefully! Please fill in the last blank.

Upon the class's completion of this task, the teacher collects student papers and evaluates students' independent spelling of target words.

Student Writing Sample

In this assessment, select a personal writing piece from the students' journals, and use it to review and assess their applications of Phase One strategies. If a student has met the learning objectives, the sample will demonstrate the standard spelling of targeted sight words in either the drafting stage or in the final, independent student editing stage.

Student Spelling Evaluation Checklist

This student evaluation checklist, with supporting assessment documentation, is a useful reference to use during parent/teacher conferences. It clarifies for parents how effectively their child is developing successful spelling strategies.

Student Spelling Evaluation Checklist for Phase One: Learning Sight Words

Name of Student _____

SKILL/STRATEGY	SKILL	SKILL	SKILL
Identify high frequency words	#correct/target	#correct/target	#correct/target
Write standard spelling of sight words in isolation	#correct/target	#correct/target	#correct/target
Write standard spelling of sight words in context	#correct/target	#correct/target	#correct/target
Write/edit standard sight words in personal writing pieces (Teacher comments)			

Name _____

Spelling Word Study Strategy

Word Study List	Look, Say, Copy (Study and then copy the word as you say it aloud.)	Cover and Write (Cover your word and try to write it all by yourself.)	Check (Check the word after you write it, and rewrite it if you need extra practice.)
	Fold here		
1.			
2.			
3.			
4.			
5.			
6.			
7.			
8.			
9.			
10.			

TWO ADDITIONAL INDEPENDENT LEARNING CENTER GAMES
FOR REINFORCING SIGHT WORDS

Name _____   Date _____

Concentration

Write your spelling words in the boxes below. Cut out the boxes and shuffle them with your partner's cards. Lay the cards face down and take turns trying to find a match.

Name _____   Date _____

Spelling Bingo

Write your spelling words in the boxes below. You may repeat your words to fill in the extra boxes. Listen to the caller. When they call a word you have, cover it with a chip. Only one word can be covered per call. The first person to have a complete row (up, down, or diagonal) wins.

		Free Space		

CHAPTER 3

Developing Phonological Skills: Rhyming and Phoneme Manipulation

PHASE TWO: NOVEMBER–DECEMBER

During Phase Two of our spelling/word study approach, we focus on the auditory sequencing aspect of spelling. Our mini-lessons in this phase highlight what good spellers listen for in texts and how they can build on their understanding of language to encode new words.

Recent research in the field of literacy has clearly established the need for children to have many experiences with phonemes in order to be successful writers. Effective spellers know how to articulate words slowly, segmenting the words into individual sounds or phonemes. Inviting students to play with and work with rhythm and rhyme gives them opportunities to enrich their language sense. Poetry provides practice in phonemic awareness, for it can help students recognize that spoken words are made up of individual sounds.

WORDS OF NOTE

"The recognition of rhyme may be the entry point to phonemic awareness development for many children."

—P.E. Bryant, 1990,
EducationNews.org

We begin Phase Two of study by regularly reading rhyming books, songs, and poems with children during Shared Reading sessions. To allow children to read and revisit favorite songs and poems during center time or independent reading sessions, we write the songs and poems on large chart paper and display them in the classroom. A typical week of word study in this phase is launched with one of the mini-lessons outlined in the chart below, followed by guided or coached practice, independent practice activities in classroom word study centers, an end-of-week "kid-watching," classroom-based assessments, and finally by Home Link assignments (see Appendix 1, pages 118–123).

WORDS OF NOTE

"Studies by Bryant, Bradley, McLean, and Crossland (1989) showed a very strong relationship between rhyming ability at age three years and performance at reading and spelling three years later."

—Dr. Kerry Hempenstall, "Phonemic Awareness: What Does It Mean?" EducationNews.org

Explicit Teaching: Modeling Strategies Through Mini-Lessons

Through the following series of mini-lessons, we draw our students' attention to what good spellers do to develop phonological skills. A typical week of word study in this phase is launched with one of the mini-lessons outlined in the chart below.

Overview of Model Mini-Lessons for Phase Two

Lesson Focusing Question	Lesson Purpose Statement
What do good spellers listen for in texts?	They listen for rhyming words.
What do good spellers look for in rhyming words?	They notice onset and rime patterns in rhyming words.
How do good spellers build new words?	They use rhyming patterns and change beginning letters. Good spellers say, "I know *my* so I can spell *by*." They change ending letters. Good spellers say, "I know *can* so I can spell *cat*." They change middle letters or vowels. Good spellers say, "I know *man*, so I can spell *men*.
How else do good spellers edit their writing?	Good spellers look and check parts of words. They check the number of parts in words. They check each part for a vowel. They check common rhyming patterns.

Mini-Lesson #1

Essential Understanding: *"What do good spellers listen for in texts?"*

"They listen for rhyming words."

Focus of Lesson: This mini-lesson draws children's attention to rhyming words—or words that have the same end sounds.

Whole-Class Instruction: Invite children to listen to several popular poems that feature rhyming elements. Ask them to identify rhyming words as you list their responses on a chart.

SAMPLE DIALOGUE:

Mrs. H.: Today, we are going to read a wonderful nursery rhyme poem called "To Market, To Market." I'd like you to listen and enjoy the rhythm as I read the poem once through. I will read the poem a second time and I would like you to listen for words that rhyme.

(Mrs. H. reads the poem twice.)

Mrs. H.: Who can tell me which words in this poem rhyme?

Whitney: *Pig* and *jig.*

Mrs. H.: Great listening, Whitney.

(Mrs. H. lists the words on chart paper.)

Mrs. H.: Did anyone hear any other rhyming words?

Jason: *Hog* and *jog.*

(Mrs. H. again lists the words on the chart paper.)

> **TO MARKET, TO MARKET**
>
> To market, to market
> To buy a fat pig
> Home again, home again,
> Jiggety, jig.
>
> To market, to market
> To buy a fat hog.
> Home again, home again,
> Jiggety, jog.
>
> —Traditional

Mrs. H.: Great listening, boys and girls. Let's take a look at the rhyming words. Who can tell me what you notice?

Lori: The words that rhyme end with the same letters—like *-ig.*

Mrs. H.: Yes, Lori. Rhyming words all end with the same sound and sometimes they <u>look</u> the same or end with the same sequence of letters.

TEACHER'S CORNER
Place highlighting tape over the sequence of letters that rhyme to draw the children's attention to the patterns.

RHYMING WORDS

pig   hog
jig   jog

Mini-Lesson #2

Essential Understanding: *"What do good spellers look for in rhyming words?"*

"They notice onset and rime patterns in rhyming words."

Focus of Lesson: This follow-up mini-lesson expands children's understanding of rhyming words by introducing them to the onset and rime patterns.

Whole-Class Instruction: Before instruction, gather lists of rhyming words and print them on chart paper. To begin the lesson, invite the children to use highlighting tape or a yellow marker to underline the rime portion (e.g. *cat*, *fat*). Explain that the letter or letters before the vowel are called the "onset" part. Share with children that good spellers notice parts of rhyming words so that they can use what they notice later when they read and write new words.

SAMPLE DIALOGUE:

Mrs. H.: Today, boys and girls, I invite you to work in pairs and search with your partners for rhyming words in books, poems, and songs around the room. Please record the rhyming words in your notebooks, and underline the rime portion using your yellow highlighters. Let's try an example together. Who can find two rhyming words on one of our poetry charts?

Brett: *Dock* and *clock.*

(Mrs. H. writes Brett's example on chart paper.)

Mrs. H.: Great example from the rhyme "Hickory, Dickory, Dock." Please come up to the chart and use your highlighter to underline the rime portion.

(Brett underlines the letters ock in both words.)

Mrs. H.: That's correct, Brett. Are there any questions? If you and your partner feel comfortable that you understand the directions, please begin your search. If not, please come meet with me to review another example.

After approximately 15–20 minutes of exploring words, bring the children back together as a group to share their discoveries. Add their work to the class "Rhyme Chart" and display this chart as a resource during Writers' Workshops.

Spelling Success in the Early Grades ● Scholastic Teaching Resources

Mini-Lesson #3

Essential Understanding: *"How do good spellers build new words?"*
"They use rhyming patterns and change beginning letters."
"Good spellers say, 'I know my, *so I can spell* by.'"
"They change ending letters."
"Good spellers say, 'I know can, *so I can spell* cat.'"
"They change middle letters or vowels."
"Good spellers say, 'I know man, *so I can spell* men.'"

Focus of Lesson: This mini-lesson demonstrates to children how they can use what they already know about words to form new words. To make this mini-lesson as effective as possible, we usually conduct it using a white magnetic board and magnetic letters.

Whole-Class Instruction: Invite children to gather together on the carpet or class meeting area, facing a large white magnetic board or chalkboard.

SAMPLE DIALOGUE:

Mrs. H.: We've been studying rhyming patterns and today we are going to use some of these familiar patterns to create new words.

(Mrs. H. uses magnetic letters to form the word pig *on the magnetic board.)*

Mrs. H: Who recognizes this word from the poem we read together entitled, "No One"?

Brett: It says *pig*.

Mrs. H.: Great. Now, how can we change this word to make it say *wig*?

Lori: You just have to change the *p* to *w*. Can I come up and do that?

Mrs. H.: Sure, Lori. As Lori is changing our word, we can think together of other familiar rhymes to play with.

(Jason raises his hand.)

Mrs. H.: Yes, Jason?

Jason: I can spell *day*, so I can change the *d* to a *p* and make it say *pay*.

Mrs. H.: Super, Jason! That's exactly what good spellers do. They use what they know to make new words.

Invite children to again work with a buddy to record common rhyming words in their notebooks. Then ask them to generate additional words by changing the beginning letters.

Related Mini-Lessons: Use the same format and approach as this mini-lesson, but focus instead on changing ending sounds and, ultimately, middle sounds to create new words. Continue to use the familiar verbal prompt, "If I know how to spell_____, then I can spell _____."

Mini-Lesson #4

Essential Understanding: *"How else do good spellers edit their writing?"*

"Good spellers look and check parts of words. They check the number of parts in words. They check each part for a vowel. They check common rhyming patterns."

Focus of Lesson: This mini-lesson helps students integrate and apply newly-taught phonological spelling strategies into their editing process. Such lessons are usually taught during Writers' Workshop sessions.

Whole-Class Instruction: Invite the class to join you as you share the pen with students for an interactive writing session. Ask children to help you finish your morning message story (see sample below).

Invite student volunteers to fill in the missing words: *wrap, family, decorate, ribbons,* and *string* on the enlarged chart paper. Explain to the class that you will edit the story together.

SAMPLE DIALOGUE:

Mrs. H.: When we edit our writing, we first must check to see if all of our words look right. Then we can check the parts of words. Does anyone notice any words in the morning message that don't look right?

Billy: The word *family* (*which has been written as* famle) doesn't look right.

Mrs. H.: We can check by first saying the word aloud and listening for the number of parts: *fam—i—ly*. How many parts did you hear?

Lori: Three parts.

(Mrs. H. draws three lines on the white board.)

Mrs. H.: Let's spell each part together: *fam—i—ly*.

(The class chorally spells: fam—i—ly.)

Mrs. H.: Let's now check to see if each part of the word has a vowel.

Lori: Yes: *a, i,* and *y. Y* can be a vowel sometimes.

December 15, 2003

Dear Children,

Today we are going to **wrap** the presents that we made for our **family** . Then we are going to **decorate** our packages with **ribbons** and **string** .

Later we will have our class holiday party.

Love,
Mrs. H.

TEACHER'S CORNER

Display the rhyming word charts around the room so that children may refer to them and use them as tools when they self-edit their writing. At the end of Writers' Workshop sessions, bring the children together for a group share and invite them to describe what strategies they used to self-edit their writing. It is important to continually reinforce and celebrate children's independent application of essential spelling/word study strategies.

Mrs. H.: Great job! Are there any other ways that you can check if we spelled this hard word correctly?

Jason: Yes. I can spell my brother's name *Sam*, so I can spell the first part of the word: *fam-*.

Mrs. H.: You are all amazing word problem solvers!

Guided Practice Activities

In this section, we offer five guided practice activities. Each activity or pair of activities accompanies a mini-lesson from the preceding section and helps students use what they just learned in the lesson. These guided practice activities are interactive experiences that will enable children to "learn how to learn" the auditory aspects of spelling. They can be used for whole-class or small-group lessons. The chart below provides an overview of the scope of these activities, their purpose, and the lessons they are intended to accompany.

Overview of Guided Practice Activities for Phase Two		
Guided Practice Activity	**Use For**	**Accompanies This Mini-Lesson**
Fun With Songs, Poems, and Books	Listening for rhyme and identifying specific rhyming patterns in texts	What do good spellers listen for in texts?
Poem Detective	Identifying onset and rime	What do good spellers look for in rhyming words?
Poem or Song/Word Play Song/Word Play Letter Cards	Changing beginning letters of words to make new words Changing middle letters (vowels) of words tomake new words	How do good spellers build new words?
Reference Tools: Class Chart	Looking and checking parts of words	How else do good spellers edit their writing?

Guided Practice Activity: FUN WITH SONGS, POEMS, AND BOOKS

Purpose: To develop an awareness of rhyme

Use for: Listening for rhyme and identifying specific rhyming patterns in texts

Materials: Poem or song on chart paper (or storybooks); easel; wooden sticks (or triangles or xylophones)

Procedure: Have available a favorite, familiar poem or song written on chart paper. Give each child a pair of wooden sticks. Invite the children to gather on the rug in front of the easel and to listen to the poem or song as you read it to them. Ask them to join in by banging their sticks together each time they hear rhyming words.

SAMPLE DIALOGUE:

Mrs. M: On my chart paper I have one of our favorite poems: "Jack and Jill"! Today I'm going to read it to you and I need you to listen very carefully. Every time you hear rhyming words in the poem, bang your sticks together. Ready?

Class: Ready.

(Mrs. M. recites the following poem.)

> Jack and Jill
> Went up the hill
> To fetch a pail of water.
> Jack fell down
> And broke his crown
> And Jill came tumbling after.

(The children bang their sticks.)

(The children bang their sticks.)

Mrs. M.: Great job! Let's try it again while I read *Green Eggs and Ham*.

WORDS OF NOTE

"There is a natural human tendency to enjoy the sounds of language. Parents and teachers can use this natural enjoyment of poetry, song, and rhyme to help young children pay close attention to how language sounds."
—Pinnell & Fountas, 1998

Guided Practice Activity: POEM DETECTIVE

Purpose: To notice onset and rime patterns in rhyming words

Use for: Identifying onset and rime

Materials: Poem written on chart paper (laminated for multiple uses); easel; two erasable markers in different colors

Procedure: Invite the class to gather around the easel. Read the poem to students as you ask them to look for onset and rime patterns within the words in the poem.

SAMPLE DIALOGUE:

Mrs. M.: Let's take a look at the poem on our chart paper. It's called "Swing!"

(Mrs. M. reads the poem to the children.)

Mrs. M.: What do you notice?

Andrew: There are a lot of -*ing* words.

Jenny: All the -*ing* words rhyme.

> **SWING!**
> Swing, swing,
> I love to swing.
> Swing, swing,
> I am a King!

Mrs. M.: Yes! Good noticing! Now take a closer look at the poem. Let's see if we can find the onset and rime of each rhyming -*ing* word. We'll begin with the words *swing, swing.* Who can tell me what the onset is?

Frank: I think it's *sw-*.

Mrs. M.: Yes, Frank. Please come up and use my red marker and circle the onset *sw-*. What is the rime?

Patricia: It's -*ing*.

Mrs. M.: Great, Patricia. Come up and circle the rime -*ing* with my blue marker. Let's continue. We are going to circle the onset in red and the rime in blue.

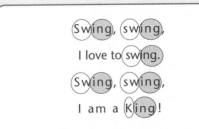

Guided Practice Activity: POEM OR SONG/WORD PLAY

Purpose: To build new words

Use for: Changing beginning letters of words to make new words

Materials: Chart Paper; easel; copy of the poem, "The Squirrel" on chart paper

Procedure: Invite the children to the rug and tell them that you are going to read a poem together.

SAMPLE DIALOGUE:

Mrs.M.: I think you're all going to enjoy the poem called "The Squirrel." Today I wrote part of that poem on my chart paper. Read along with me while I point to the words. Ready?

Children: Ready!

> **THE SQUIRREL**
>
> Whisky, frisky
> Hippity, hop
> Up he goes
> To the tree top!
>
> Whirly, twirly,
> Round and round,
> Down he scampers
> To the ground.
>
> Furly, curly,
> What a tail!
> Tall as a feather,
> Broad as a sail!
>
> Where's his supper?
> In the shell,
> Snappity, crackity,
> Out it fell!
>
> —Anonymous

TEACHER'S CORNER
Management Tip

One way to build on students' knowledge of sounds in words is through song. Songs let children experiment with sound in an easy, non-threatening way. Using songs is therefore a good way to engage children, and this is especially true if the song is already familiar. For instance, if they already know the lyrics to a song, students can more easily read along when they see it written on chart paper. So it's a good idea to play the song you use for this activity a few times before starting. For example, sometimes we use Raffi's "Down by the Bay" at snack time or recess, or when students are working. Playing the tape and providing copies of the book in a listening center is helpful, too.

Mrs. M: Wow! What great readers you are! Today we're going to take a closer look at this poem. Did anyone notice anything about it?

Andrew: It rhymes!

Mrs. M: It sure does. I'm going to read it again and every time you hear a rhyme, I'd like you to clap your hands.

Mrs. M: I noticed that you clapped for a lot of different rhymes. Two of them were *round* and *ground* and *sail* and *tail*. Why did you clap for them?

Kevin: *Round* and *ground* rhyme because they both have *-ound* as the rime.

Patty: And *-ail* is the rime in *sail* and *tail*.

Mrs. M.: Good noticing! Now let's use that information to help us become better spellers. If you're writing in your journals and you're unsure of how to spell a word, sometimes you can use what you already know to help you write that word. I'll show you how.

Let's look at *sail* again. I can change the beginning letter to *t* to spell the word *tail*.

(Mrs. M. writes the words sail *and* tail *on chart paper in order for children to visualize what she is saying.)*

Now you try. If I know how to spell *sail* and *tail*, how would I spell *pail*?

Frank: Change the *s* to a *p*.

Mrs. M.: Excellent!

Mrs. M.: Now let's look at *hop* and *top*. If I know them, then how can I write *mop*?

Chris: Change the first letter to an *m*.

(Mrs. M. continues to make new words with the children, such as bop *and* pop.)*

Mrs. M: Wonderful! Now you're getting it! So when you're writing and you get stuck on a word, see if you can spell new words by changing the first letter.

Variation: A song that works really well for this activity is "Oh-A-Hunting We Will Go."

THE SQUIRREL

Whisky, frisky
Hippity, **hop**
Up he goes
To the tree **top!**

Whirly, twirly,
Round and **round,**
Down he scampers
To the **ground.**

Furly, curly,
What a **tail!**
Tall as a feather,
Broad as a **sail!**

Where's his supper?
In the **shell,**
Snappity, crackity,
Out it **fell!**

—Anonymous

(Students clap.)

(Students clap.)

(Students clap.)

(Students clap.)

(Students clap.)

(Students clap.)

(Students clap.)

WORDS OF NOTE

"The challenge is to find ways to get children to notice the phonemes, to discover their existence and separability. Fortunately, many of the activities involving rhyme, rhythm, listening, and sounds that have long been enjoyed with preschool-age children are ideally suited for this purpose."

—Jager Adams, Foorman, Lundberg, and Beeler, 1998

Spelling Success in the Early Grades ● Scholastic Teaching Resources

Guided Practice Activity: SONG/WORD PLAY

Purpose: To build new words

Use for: Changing middle letters (vowels) of words to make new words

Materials: Chart paper; easel; the song, "Change the Sound," written on chart paper; marker

Procedure: Write the lyrics to "Change the Sound" on chart paper.

Gather students on the rug and sing the song together several times. Then invite children to change a word's middle sound.

> **CHANGE THE SOUND**
> (to be sung to the tune of "Row, Row, Row Your Boat")
> Change, change, change the sound
> Change the sound around.
> Take the *a* and make it *u*
> A new word you have found.

SAMPLE DIALOGUE:

Mrs. M.: Let's fiddle around with the word *cat*.

(Mrs. M. writes the word on chart paper.)

Mrs. M.: Let's change the middle sound to a /u/.

(Mrs. M. writes the new word on the chart paper.)

What's our new word?

Class: Cut.

(Mrs. M. continues this process using other words and having as many volunteers as possible come up with their own examples.)

Variations: You can also use this activity very effectively with the songs "Abiyoyo," sung by Pete Seeger and "Willoughby Wallaby Woo," sung by Raffi.

Guided Practice Activity: LETTER CARDS

Purpose: To build new words

Use for: Changing ending letters of words to make new words

Materials and Preparation: Pocket chart; letter cards made from index cards or card stock; markers (1 red and 1 black). To prepare for this activity, cut out several rectangles from card stock, or use index cards measuring $2\frac{1}{2}$ x 3 inches. To create the letter cards, write the desired letters on the top portion of the cards. To differentiate between vowels and consonants, use different colored markers. In our activity, vowels are written in red and consonants are written in blue.

Procedure: Gather the children around a pocket chart and invite them to make words.

SAMPLE DIALOGUE:

Mrs. M.: Today we are going to build some words. To help out, we're going to use these letter cards and my pocket chart. Let's take a look at them.

(She displays the letter cards c, a, t, n, r, p, *and* b.*)*

What do you notice?

Mary: One letter is red and all the other ones are blue.

Susie: The red one is a vowel.

Mrs. M.: Good noticing! The *a* is a vowel and it's written in red to remind you of that. Vowels are like the glue that holds words together. Every word must have at least one vowel in it. So all of the words we're going to build today will have the letter *a* in it. Let's build the word *cat*. Which letters will we use?

John: C, *a,* and *t*.

Mrs. M.: Okay, John. Come up and build the word *cat* with the cards.

Mrs. M.: Now if I change the ending letter to another letter, I can make the word *car*. How can I do that?

Sarah: Change the *t* to an *r*.

Mrs. M.: Good work. Come up and do that.

(Mrs. M. continues by making the words can, cap, *and* cab.*)*

Extension: Depending on the children's grade level and their success with this activity, you can use two vowels on a letter card. The children can manipulate beginning, middle, and ending letters to build new words.

Suggested sets of letters to write on the letter cards are:

Letter cards:
c a t n r p b
Words to make:
cat, can, car, cap, cab

Letter cards:
p o t p w d
Words to make:
pot, pop, pow, pod

Letter cards:
s i p t r s n
Words to make:
sip, sit, sir, sis, sin

WORDS OF NOTE

"Making words is a powerful activity because within one instructional format there are endless possibilities for discovering how our alphabetic system works."
—Cunningham & Cunningham, 1992

Guided Practice Activity: REFERENCE TOOLS: CLASS CHART

Purpose: To edit writing

Use for: Looking and checking parts of words

Materials: Chart paper; easel; marker; journal entry

Procedure: Invite a child to choose an entry from his or her journal to share with the class. Without changing anything, copy the entry on chart paper and post it on the easel.

SAMPLE DIALOGUE:

Mrs. M.: David was kind enough to share one of his journal entries with us, and I copied it on my chart paper. Our job today is to help David with his editing. Let's think about what good spellers do to edit their writing.

Mary: Good spellers look and check parts of words.

Sally: Good spellers check the number of parts in words.

Molly: Good spellers check each part for a vowel.

Danny: Good spellers check rhyming patterns.

(Mrs. M. writes these tips on chart paper to create a class checklist, or editing rubric.)

Mrs. M.: Yes, good spellers do all of these things. I wrote down all that you said. The tips you gave me are going to become part of a checklist. We can also call this our editing rubric. We're going to use this rubric when editing our work. Now let's take a look at David's entry and see if we can help him. David is going to read it to us.

(David reads the entry.)

Mrs. M.: David, which words were tricky for you to write?

David: I think I spelled *important* wrong. And *presents*, too.

Mrs. M.: Okay. Let's take a look. Which rules on our checklist can we use to check the word *important*?

Shari: We can check the number of parts in the word and check each part for a vowel.

Mrs. M.: Okay. Let's clap out the word important: *im-por-tant*.
How many parts did you hear?

Class: Three.

Mrs. M.: Yes, there are three. Let's draw the three parts.

Now let's do the first part: *im-*.

Mary: It's just like *am*, but with an *i.*]

Mrs. M.: *-por-*

Michael: *p, o, r*

> **David's Journal Draft Entry:**
> Today I am going to my Grandma's house. I am so happy. It is a very imprtnt day becos it is her brthday. We are going to hav cak. We are going to open prsentz. I can't wait.

TEACHER'S CORNER

If you edit every single aspect of a child's journal entry, not only will it be too laborious for children, but they will lose confidence in their writing. For errors in basic sight words such as *have* and *because*—words that were misspelled in David's entry—remind children to check the word wall or their personal dictionaries.

Mrs. M.: *-tant*

Marissa: *t, a, n, t*

Mrs. M.: Wow! Look at that big word you spelled!

> *(Mrs. M continues to follow this process, primarily with the words from the journal entry that David identified as being tricky.)*

Extension: Invite children to choose one entry from their own journals to edit using the checklist posted on the chart. You can also type up the checklist and instruct children to keep them in their journals to use as a resource while they are writing.

Independent Practice: Learning Center Activities

After mini-lessons and guided practice, provide students with an opportunity to explore a range of hands-on activities that reinforce their rhyming skills and their phoneme manipulation of words. The following learning center activities offer young children independent practice in word study strategies. As you can see from the diagram above, these activities are far along the spectrum of decreasing levels of teacher support. Each activity includes a period of modeling and instruction—essentially, an introduction to the activity. After this introduction, place the activity in a learning center and make it available to the class. It is here that the independent learning takes place. As in Chapter 2, the activities are balanced to take into account the different learning styles that young children bring to the classroom.

Overview of Independent Practice Activities for Phase Two

Independent Practice Activity	Learning Style Connection	Purpose
Listening for Rhymes in Poems and Songs	Musical and Linguistic	Good spellers listen for rhyming words in text.
Noticing Onset and Rime in Text	Linguistic	Good spellers can find onset and rime in rhyming words.
Making New Rhymes: Changing the Beginning Sound	Linguistic	Good spellers say, "I know *by* so I can spell *my*."
Building New Words: Changing the Ending Sound	Linguistic	Good spellers say, "I know *can* so I can spell *cat*."
Change the Sound and Word Plays	Musical and Linguistic	Good spellers can change the middle (vowel) sound."I know *man* so I can spell *men*."
Using Rhythm Sticks to Recognize Word Parts	Musical and Linguistic	Good spellers can listen and look for the parts of words. They check each beat for a vowel.
Becoming Good Editors	Linguistic	Good spellers look and check for parts of words, number of parts, and they check the part for a vowel sound.

Independent Practice Activity:
LISTENING FOR RHYMES IN POEMS AND SONGS

Learning Style: Musical and Linguistic

Purpose: To listen for and identify rhyming words in songs, stories, and poems

Materials: Recordings of rhyming songs such as "There Was an Old Woman Who Swallowed a Fly" and poems such as "Jumping Monkeys"; a good listening center with individual earphones for 7 or 8 students; one photocopy of "There Was an Old Woman" and "Jumping Monkeys" for each child in the learning center; popsicle sticks; crayons; and paper

Modeling and Introduction: Remind the students of how they listened to poems and rhymes in the guided instruction activity. Tell the class that one of their independent activities today will involve listening to a rhyming song called "There Was an Old Woman Who Swallowed a Fly."

SAMPLE DIALOGUE:

Ms. K.: As you listen to the story on the recording, put down a popsicle stick for each set of rhyming words that you hear. When the recording is finished, compare the number of rhymes you heard with the number that the other children in your group heard. Then see how many of the rhymes you can remember.

(Once the children have done this, Ms. K. continues.)

Ms. K.: Take a copy of the song and listen to it again. See how many of the rhymes you can find on your song copy and circle them with your crayon. Turn the recording off and compare the words you have circled with those that your group members circled.

If you feel that your students need further teacher-directed instruction, repeat the same procedure with "Jumping Monkeys." If not, use "Jumping Monkeys" in the learning center as one of the activities set up for independent work.

Learning Center Activity: Once the whole class has become familiar with the procedure, they are ready to practice it as an independent activity in their word study centers. It is a good idea to have a parent volunteer help with this activity at the initial stage.

> ### THERE WAS AN OLD WOMAN
>
> There was an old woman who swallowed a fly.
> I wonder why
> She swallowed that fly.
> Perhaps she'll die.
>
> There was an old woman who swallowed a spider
> That wriggled and jiggled
> And squiggled
> Inside her.
>
> She swallowed the spider to
> Catch the fly.
> I wonder why
> She swallowed that fly.
> Perhaps she'll die.
>
> (verses continue through bat, bird, cow and horse)
>
> —Traditional

TEACHER'S CORNER

It's a good idea to instruct students ahead of time about how to operate the audio equipment, whether a cassette tape player, CD player, or MP3 player. Write these instructions on a chart and mount it near the listening center.

Extension: A related center activity is to ask students to make drawings for one of the rhymes in "Down by the Bay" or another rhythmic poem.

Independent Practice Activity: NOTICING ONSET AND RIME IN TEXT

Learning Style: Linguistic

Purpose: To identify onset and rime in rhyming words

Materials: The poem, "Swing!" written on chart paper; one photocopy of the poems "Almost Lunchtime" and "Higglety, Pigglety, Pop!" for each child (6–10) at a learning center; crayons and highlighter markers (demonstrate use of highlighters if children have not used them before)

Modeling and Introduction: To refresh the work students have done in their previous guided practice activity, introduce the center activity by showing them the poem "Swing!" (written on a chart). Call on children to identify the onset of the rime in the rhyming words.

SAMPLE DIALOGUE:

Ms. K.: Today one of your center activities will be to look at two poems, "Almost Lunchtime" and "Higglety, Pigglety, Pop!" I'm going to read the poems to you, and I want to see if you can tell me which words rhyme in each poem.

(Ms. K. reads one poem at a time and each time asks the students to name the rhyming pairs.)

Ms. K.: Which part of the word sounds the same in *mop* and *pop*?

Samantha: The /op/ sound.

Ms. K.: Yes! You know what to do now. Each person in the center will have a copy of each poem and crayons and highlighter pens. Read the poems together and circle the rhyming words with a crayon. What do think you will do with the highlighter pens?

Jake: I bet we'll use them to mark the parts of the rhymes that look or sound the same. That's always the ending letter sounds.

Learning Center Activity: Once the whole class has become familiar with the procedure, they are ready to practice it as an independent activity in their word study centers. To help them get started, suggest that they should compare with each other the parts of the rhyming words that show onset and rhyme. As needed, make available additional rhyming poems. The children can illustrate the poems when they have completed the activity.

ALMOST LUNCHTIME

I could eat
a great big bunch
of chips and salsa
for my lunch,
and
top it off
with fruity punch,
and then some more chips.
crunch, crunch, crunch!
　　　　—Helen H. Moore

HIGGLETY, PIGGLETY, POP!

Higglety,
Pigglety,
Pop!
The dog has eaten the mop;
The pig's in a hurry,
The cat's in a flurry.
Higglety, pigglety, pop!

　　　　—Traditional

Spelling Success in the Early Grades • Scholastic Teaching Resources

Independent Practice Activity:
MAKING NEW RHYMES: CHANGING THE BEGINNING SOUND

Learning Style: Linguistic

Purpose: To recognize rhyming patterns and build new words

Materials: "Down by the Bay" book and song; paper, pencils, and crayons for 5 to 8 students

Modeling and Introduction: Invite the children to sit on the class rug. Remind the students that in their guided practice activity, they changed the beginning sounds of the rhyming words in the poem, "The Squirrel." Tell them that today they will be using the familiar song, "Down by the Bay."

SAMPLE DIALOGUE:

Ms. K.: Let's remember and say some of the new rhyming words we made by changing the beginning letter in "The Squirrel." Now let's do that with a song we all know, "Down by the Bay." *(As the children sing through the song, Ms. K. stops at the part: "Did you ever see a cat sitting on a _____.")* Who can make a new word that rhymes with *cat* by changing the beginning letter sound?

Britinni: I know one: "Did you ever see a cat sitting on a purple hat, down by the bay."

(Other students wave their hands in the air, eager to share new rhymes.)

Kevin: "Did you ever see a lark running after a shark, down by the bay."

Learning Center Activity: Tell children that one of the independent learning centers today will be to come up with new rhymes by changing beginning letter sounds. Have students draw funny pictures about their rhymes and write the new rhymes underneath their drawings. Remind them to use lots of details in their pictures and to color carefully. When you feel certain that students are familiar and comfortable with the procedure, make this word study center available.

Extension: Once everyone in the class has had a chance to engage in this center activity, ask children to assemble their pictures and rhymes into a class book. Have them take turns bringing the class book home to share with their families.

Independent Practice Activity:
BUILDING NEW WORDS: CHANGING THE ENDING SOUND

Learning Style: Linguistic

Purpose: To change the ending sound of words to build new words

Materials and Preparation: Teacher-made individual letter pockets; teacher-made alphabet letter cards (one set per student in a center) to fit into the pockets. Make the letter pockets by folding a piece of oaktag paper the long way and stapling it on two ends to create a mini-pocket chart. For the individual letter cards, print one letter on each card to fit into the pocket. Write the vowels in one color and the consonants in another. (See page 70.)

Modeling and Introduction: Remind the students that good spellers are able to change the beginning, middle, and ending letters in words to build new words.

c	a	n

SAMPLE DIALOGUE:

Ms. K.: We have a new learning center activity today. But first I want to introduce it to you.

(As the students sit on the rug around her, she shows them the little pocket chart and the small individual letter cards. She points out that the cards can be used to build words, and that the children have used these already in the sight word activity centers).

What do you notice about these cards?

Liam: The vowels are a different color than the consonant letters.

Ms. K.: Yes, that's right! How can we change *can* into *cat*? *(She demonstrates the word building process by having a volunteer build the word* can *in the pocket chart. Other children come forward to build different words by changing the ending sounds.)*

Changing the beginnings and endings of words can be reinforced in many ways, including this fun way of using shaving cream.

Learning Center Activity: Students are now ready to go to the centers to build words. The word study centers can focus on changing the beginning letter sounds and the middle letter vowel sound to build new words, or can offer different opportunities to work with the ending sounds. Six to eight students make a good-sized group for this center. It's also helpful to have a parent volunteer assist in the beginning stages.

Extension Activity: The children in the centers write down all of the new words they have created and share them with the class, presenting first the original word and then the word they built.

Independent Practice Activity:
CHANGE THE SOUND AND WORD PLAYS

Learning Style: Musical and Linguistic

Purpose: To learn to hear the change in the middle vowel sound

Materials: The Story of Abiyoyo, based on an African Folk Tale retold by Pete Seeger; recordings of "Abiyoyo" and "Miss Mary Mack"

Modeling and Introduction: Remind the children of the song "Change the Sound" and the procedure they learned in that guided practice activity for changing the middle vowel sound in a word. Tell them that today you are going to read the African folk tale "Abiyoyo." While you read aloud, help the children learn the book's recurring song. Have the class sing it together—just as the little boy and the giant Abiyoyo do in the story.

Next, ask the children to clap the syllables in Abiyoyo. Play a word game with them: Have them say Abiyoyo's name and then repeat it again without the *Abi-*. They should correctly respond: *yoyo*. Then ask them to say *Abiyoyo*, substituting long *e* for *o*: They respond *Abiyeye*! Continue this word and sound play by asking how the name would sound with *u*, then *a*, then *i* (all long vowel sounds). The children sing the song, each time using a different vowel sound.

> Abiyoyo, Abiyoyo
> Abiyoyo, Abiyoyo
> Abiyoyo, ya, yo, yo ya, yo, yo

Finally, ask them to try different consonant sounds in front of *Abiyoyo* to make more word plays: *Babiyoyo, Habiyoyo, Tabiyoyo*, etc.

Learning Center Activity: This listening learning center works well with no more than six students at a time. Once they have learned the procedure, allow them to listen to audio tapes of "Abiyoyo," "Miss Mary Mack," and "The Wheels on the Bus," substituting middle vowel sounds in the words of these songs.

For "The Wheels on the Bus," ask students to make vowel changes such as: "The babies on the bus went whee, whee, whee" instead of "waa, waa, waa," and so on. For "Miss Mary Mack," ask children to substitute sounds as follows: "Miss Mary Mack, Mack, Mack/All dressed in Black, Black, Black" can become "Miss Mary Meeck, Meeck, Meeck/ All dressed in Bleeck Bleeck, Bleeck," and so on.

Independent Practice Activity:
USING RHYTHM STICKS TO RECOGNIZE WORD PARTS

Learning Style: Musical and Linguistic

Purpose: To discriminate the parts of words in songs and rhymes

Materials: Rhythm sticks or individual xylophones; word wall or word cards with sight words printed on them

Modeling and Introduction: Tell students that in this activity they are going to use musical instruments—rhythm sticks or xylophones—to tap out the number of syllables that they hear in individual words.

Children enjoy using rhythm sticks to tap out syllables.

SAMPLE DIALOGUE:

Ms. K. *(singing or saying)*: What's your name, little girl?

Leah: My name is *Le - ah*. *(As she says her name, Leah uses sticks to mark the syllables. The rest of the group repeats her name and taps out the syllables with the sticks:* Le - ah.*)*

Leah: What's your name, little boy? *(She points to another child.)*

Daniel: My name is *Dan - iel*. *(As he speaks, he hits the sticks together, marking the number of syllables in* Dan-iel.*)*

(The group repeats the name and hits the sticks with the correct number of syllables.)

Ms. K. *(extending the activity to sight words from the word wall)*: What's your word, David?

David: My word is *play-ing*. *(He hits the sticks for the correct number of syllables as he says the word.)*

(Finally, each child chooses different words and uses sticks to make the number of syllables.)

Learning Center Activity: The center activity is identical to that modeled. Once children are familiar with the procedure, they are free to engage in this center, where they choose words and the group repeats the words and indicates syllables with the rhythm sticks.

Variation: An alternate center might include a set of the sight word cards—all of the one- and two-syllable words that are on the word wall and that have been introduced in mini-lessons. Have children start this activity by saying their names and having a partner use the rhythm sticks to beat out the parts of the name as they say it. Then have one child hold up a sight word card (the children can take turns being card holders) and the rest of the group beat the number of parts with the rhythm sticks as they repeat the word. Then ask children to sort the word cards into piles according to the number of beats they hear.

Extension: Extend this activity by having children use xylophones. Have them learn to hit an adjacent note for each syllable in a word and then slide the notes together and say the word again. For example: they hit two adjacent notes for *play-ing*, then slide the notes together and say each part slowly but fluidly: *playing*.

Independent Practice Activity: BECOMING GOOD EDITORS

Learning Style: Linguistic

Purpose: To examine and check one's own writing to make sure that each word has the correct number of syllables and that each syllable has a vowel sound; to check for common rhyming patterns; to develop and use an editing rubric for checking and correcting journal writing

Materials: For each child at a center, one copy of brief journal entries that have been volunteered by the student writers themselves; pencils and white correction tape (wide size); a rubric chart (see below) displaying what to look for in written work

Modeling and Introduction: Remind the class that they have already learned in their guided practice activity how to check their writing for number of parts, for vowels in each word part, and for rhyming patterns. During morning message, reinforce the guided activity. Make deliberate errors in the message you print on the easel. Then encourage the class to notice and correct the errors. Help them check words for the correct number of parts and check word parts for vowels.

Learning Center Activity: This center works well with six to eight children, and with a parent volunteer monitoring students' work. Ms. K. explains the directions for this center in this way: "During this center activity, you will work as editors.

Your Editing Rubric

⊙ Look at the word, say it, and then clap the number of parts you hear. Does the word have enough parts?

⊙ Check the word again to see if each word part has a vowel.

⊙ Check for rhyming patterns and circle them.

You will have two journal entries each. You may work together with a partner on these to check words according to the editing rubric (see page 72) we made earlier. Read the journal entry with a partner. Use your pencil to circle the words that need to be corrected. Check with a partner to see if he or she agrees with your choices. Then go back and use your white tape. Carefully place a piece of white tape over the words and write the correction on it with your pencil." Students follow these directions and use the rubric on page 72 as they work at this center.

Teacher Assessment of Student Learning

Just as in Phase One, assessment of lessons and activities in Phase Two is best accomplished through the informal means of kid watching, maintaining an observations log, and administering brief classroom-based measures—all within the context of the instructional process. Below we examine how you can implement these assessment procedures specifically for Phase Two instruction.

ONGOING ASSESSMENT

During guided and independent practice activities, we recommend that you record both students' successes and their confusions on a daily basis. These running observations are an invaluable aid in the overall assessment of children's essential phonological awareness skills (e.g., the ability to recognize and generate rhyming patterns, the ability to manipulate phonemes within words, and so on).

Observations Log

We recommend that you use the Observation Log presented in Chapter 2 to record your observations. Each day, you might observe a small group of students and use a simple checklist to record their attainment of desired skills. Record the data and then use the key to note stages of students' skill development (e.g. pre-emerging, emerging, or secure). A completed classroom log can serve as a rich source of information for identifying which students have mastered instructional goals and which students need additional support. On page 74 we provide a completed log page for Phase Two in Ms. Varrone's first-grade class.

SPECIFIC CLASSROOM-BASED ASSESSMENTS

The following three specific classroom-based assessment tools will provide you with instructionally helpful information for this phase.

Phonological Awareness Assessment

Administer this quick assessment of the key phonological awareness understandings that are essential to spelling success (page 75) and record the results on the Student Spelling Checklist (page 74).

Contextual Dictation

Research has consistently demonstrated that phonemic segmentation is a strong predictor of spelling ability (K. Nation and C. Hulme, Reading Research Quarterly, June, 1997). Thus, using as a model the successful Dictation Test developed by Reading Recovery teachers Susan

Class Log—Observations of Phonological Skills Development

Key: (P): pre-emerging, (E): emerging, (S): secure

Names	Date(s)	Rhyming Words	Syllables	Phoneme Manipulation
Group 1				
1. Eileen		S	S	S
2. Pam	12/10	E	E	E
3. Gina		E	E	E
4. Debbie		S	S	S
5. Tracey		E	E	E
Group 2				
6. Noah		S	E	E
7. Andrew	12/11	S	E	E
8. Jonas		S	E	E
9. Lori		E	P	P
10. Jason		E	P	E
Group 3				
11. Whitney		P	P	P
12. Brett	12/12	P	E	P
13. Linda		P	P	P
14. Peter		E	E	E
15. Kevin		E	P	P
16. Danielle		S	E	E
17. Billy		E	E	E
18. Christopher		S	S	S

Student Spelling Checklist: Learning Phonological Skills

Name of child _____   Date: _____

(P): pre-emerging   (E): emerging   (S): secure

_____ Child listens for and identifies rhyming words.

_____ Child identifies onset and rime patterns in words.

_____ Child uses rhyme patterns to build new words.

_____ Child changes beginning letters to build new words.

_____ Child changes ending letters to build new words.

_____ Child changes middle letters (vowels) to build new words.

_____ Child identifies the number of syllables in words.

Spelling Success in the Early Grades • Scholastic Teaching Resources

Phonological Awareness Assessment

Name of child _____ Date _____

1. Identifies rhyming words

Teacher prompt: "Do these words rhyme?"

hat fat   boy toy   his him   big bag   fun run

2. Identifies onset and rime patterns

Teacher prompt : "Repeat the word _____, and then separate the word into its onset and rime. For example, say the word *cat,* then say *c—at.*"

pop (p—op)   man (m—an)   hill (h—ill)   play (pl—ay)
rat (r—at)   cup (c—up)   pit (p—it)   ten   (t—en)

3. Uses rhyming patterns to build new words

Teacher prompt: "What words can you name that rhyme with_____? For example, what word rhymes with *like?*" (Answer: *bike*) What rhymes with: *look, man, way, pop, pin, hen, bug, hill*?

4. Changes beginning letters to build new words

Teacher prompt: "Change the first sound in the word _____ to the _____ sound. What is the new word? For example, change the first sound in the word *car* to the /f/ sound. What is the new word?" (Answer: *far*)

<u>m</u>an /p/ sound (*pan*)   <u>f</u>ox /b/ sound (*box*)
<u>r</u>ug /t/ sound (*tug*)   <u>s</u>it /f/sound (*fit*)

5. Changes ending letters to build words

Teacher prompt: "Change the ending sound in the word _____ to the _____ sound. What is the new word? For example, change the ending sound in the word *big* to the /t/ sound. What is the new word?" (Answer: *bit*)

be<u>d</u> /t/ sound (*bet*)   bu<u>g</u> /s/ sound (*bus*)
ho<u>t</u> /p/ sound (*hop*)   ti<u>p</u> /n/ sound (*tin*)

6. Changes middle letters (vowels) to build new words

Teacher prompt: "Change the middle sound in the word _____ to the _____ sound. What is the new word? For example, change the middle sound in the word *men* to the /a/sound. What is the new word?" (Answer: *man*)

t<u>o</u>p /a/ sound (*tap*)   b<u>i</u>g /u/ sound (*bug*)
f<u>u</u>n /a/sound (*fan*)   b<u>a</u>d /e/ sound (*bed*)

7. Identifies the number of syllables in words

Teacher prompt: "How many parts do you hear in the word _____? For example, how many parts do you hear in the word *dragon?*" (Answer: 2 parts)

umbrella (3)   *bottom* (2)   *eat* (1)
monster (2)   *wonderful* (3)   *candle* (2)

Additional comments:

_____

_____

_____

Robinson and Barbara Watson (*The Early Detection of Reading Difficulties*, Marie Clay, 1979), we created this two-sentence dictation to assess students' segmentation skills. We recommend that teachers administer this dictation test in small groups or to the whole class.

In this assessment, 33 sound-to-letter associations are assessed. Silent letters (e.g., the *e* at the end of the word *take*, the *h* in the word *school*, and the *a* in the word *read*) are not counted. Vowel digraphs (e.g., *-oo-*) are counted as one sound. The purpose of this assessment is to ascertain how easily students segment words and record their corresponding sounds—an essential spelling strategy. You can also use it to assess how students are recording high-frequency vocabulary words (e.g., *go, I, to, on, and*).

Here is a completed test, showing one first-grader's response and his teacher's analysis.

SAMPLE DICTATION TEST

> Adam
>
> I go to scol on a big bos. I tak a book and I red.
>
> ---
>
> Score: 31/33
> Errors: substituted *o* for *oo* in school—remember the omission of the letter *h* does
>   not count for scoring purposes
>   Substituted *o* for *u* in bus
> Note : *red* for *read* is counted as three correct phonemes

Student Writing Sample

As in Phase One, again select sample journal entries for assessment. In this phase, assess students' independent application of phonological awareness strategies: are they encoding phonetically regular words correctly? What sound/letter confusions may still be troubling some students? Are they including multiple syllables within polysyllabic words?

The writing samples are a wonderful window into students' thinking about spelling and word study. They also are the best examples of independent applications of learned strategies. Below is one kindergartner's writing sample and a teacher analysis.

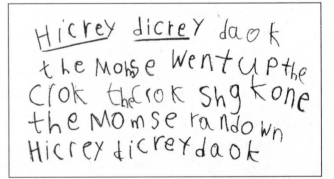

Teacher analysis: After reviewing the sample, Mrs. Varrone documented the student's attempted use of rhyming patterns to build new words.

Building Words: Using Visual, Auditory, and Meaning Features of Known Words to Make New Words

PHASE THREE: JANUARY–MARCH

In the previous two chapters, we have seen how good spellers draw upon their knowledge of common sight words and word parts, and how they use auditory/sound segmentation skills to "build" new words and to encode words. In Phase Three, we focus on how good spellers must learn how to combine known high-frequency words to form compound words, and use known meaningful parts of words (morphemes) to spell more complex, multi-syllabic words.

During Phase Three, we teach students how to use known parts of words—along with morphemes and several basic, essential spelling rules—to make informed spelling decisions. By adding familiar prefixes (e.g., *re-*, *un-*, *mis-*) and suffixes (e.g., *-ing*, *-er*, *-ful*) to common base words, good spellers can logically deduce the spelling of clusters of additional words.

As children begin to progress through the following series of mini-lessons, we notice that their "incorrect spellings" become less random in nature and begin to reflect their acquired spelling logic or knowledge of known auditory, visual, and meaning features of words, and the essential spelling rules that regulate our written English language system.

"In English, most words that have the same meaning base are spelled the same...This knowledge of the structure of words and the meaning function of different parts of words can greatly help children learn to spell."

— *Spelling Resource Book*, p. 85, developed by the Education Department of Western Australia, Heinemann, 1997

"Some children seem to get 'stuck' in the Phonetic Phase of spelling development. These children usually have a sound understanding of graphophonic relationships but have not developed any alternative strategies that they can apply when a graphophonic strategy is not appropriate. One of the major strategies that they need to develop is the use of common letter patterns which characterize the spelling of English words...Children need to be taught to look for and focus on the highly predictable sequential letter patterns of English."

— *Spelling Resource Book*, p. 84, developed by the Education Department of Western Australia, Heinemann, 1997

Explicit Teaching: Modeling Strategies Through Mini-Lessons

Through the following series of mini-lessons, we draw our students' attention to what good spellers do to learn sight words. A typical week of word study in Phase Three launches with one of the mini-lessons outlined in the chart below.

Model Mini-Lessons for Phase Three

Lesson Focusing Question	Lesson Purpose Statement
What do good spellers do to build new words?	They add, delete, and/or substitute letters within words to build on and expand their core of known words.
How else do good spellers build new words?	They join known words to form compound words.
What is something else good spellers do to build new words?	They add common syllables to the beginning (i.e. prefixes) and/or ending (i.e. suffixes) of words to alter the meaning of words.
What do good spellers use to build words?	They use five important spelling rules to build new words. • They always put a *u* after *q*. • They know that every syllable has a vowel or *y*. • They know that the silent *e* drops when adding endings that begin with a vowel. • They double consonants at the end of some words before adding an ending that begins with a vowel. • They change *y* to *i* when adding the endings *-er*, *-est*, *-ed*, or *-s* (*-es*).
How else do good spellers edit their writing?	Good spellers refer to classroom spelling charts and personal dictionaries, which list common prefixes, suffixes, and important spelling rules.

Mini-Lesson #1

Essential Understanding: *"What do good spellers do to build new words?"*

"They add, delete and/or substitute letters within words to build on and expand their core of known words."

Focus of Lesson: This mini-lesson engages children in word building to foster their attention to the common features of visually similar words—for example, *the/then, of/off, for/or,* and *come/some.*

Whole-Class Instruction: Invite children to join you at the front of the room and have them sit closely around an easel. (Alternately, have them remain at their seats and use an overhead projector to demonstrate.) Write the familiar sight word *the* in large letters on the chart or overhead transparency.

Mrs. H.: Who can read this important sight word?

(All of the children's hands rise seemingly at once.)

Mrs. H.: Please all read it together.

Children: *the*

Mrs. H.: That's correct. Now watch what happens when I add the letter *n* to the end of the word *the.* Now what new word did I spell?

Lori: You spelled *then.*

Mrs. H.: Yes, Lori. We can add letters to other words to create many additional words.

(Mrs. H. then continues to demonstrate, adding letters to three more words: you—your, he—here, *and* of—off. *Next she demonstrates deleting letters from known words:* for—or, can—an. *Finally, she models substituting letters within known words:* come—some—same.*)*

Mini-Lesson #2

Essential Understanding: *"How else do good spellers build new words?"*

"They join known words to form compound words."

Focus of Lesson: This mini-lesson heightens children's awareness of compound words.

Whole-Class Instruction: Ahead of time, write the following poem in large print on chart paper and display it for the whole class. (The print should be large enough to allow all of the children to see the text features.) During a Shared Reading lesson, invite the children to chorally recite the poem.

Notice that the poem contains several compound words:

SAMPLE DIALOGUE:

Mrs. H.: Today we are going to read aloud a wonderful poem about fireflies. It is called "Flashlights in the Dark."

flash/lights	glow/worm
bug/land	every/where
summer/time	high/ways

Mrs. H.: There are several compound words that

the poet Frances Gorman Risser has selected to use in this poem. Who can tell me what a compound word is?

Jason: A word that is made up of two little words.

Mrs. H.: Yes, Jason. Now let's all look carefully at the text and see if we can find some examples of compound words.

(Several children raise their hands.)

Whitney: *Summertime* is a compound word. There are two words that make up the one long word: *summer* and *time*.

Mrs. H.: Great! Who can find another example?

(Mrs. H. circles the compound words on the chart paper as the children identify them.)

Follow-Up Lesson: Create sets of sight word cards using the high-frequency words previously studied (e.g., *in, to, can, not, out, side, day,* etc.). Invite children to combine these familiar sight words to create compound words. After the new compound words have been formed (e.g., *into, cannot, today, outside*), have the students display them in the pocket chart.

> **FLASHLIGHTS IN THE DARK**
>
> When darkness falls in summertime,
> The avenues of air
> Are full of glowworm motor cops.
> They're zipping everywhere.
>
> With flashlights snapping on and off,
> They signal Left! Or Right!
> Directing Bugland traffic jams
> On highways of the night!
>
> —Frances Gorman Risser, *Perfect Poems for Teaching Phonics,* Scholastic Inc.

can | not

to | day

in | to

TEACHER'S CORNER
Management Tip

After writing the poems on large chart paper, we usually laminate the paper so that we can circle the compound words with washable marker. This allows us to re-use the poetry charts year after year.

Mini-Lesson #3

Essential Understanding: *"What is something else good spellers do to build new words?"*

"They add common syllables to the beginning (i.e. prefixes) and/or ending (i.e. suffixes) of words to alter the meaning of words.

Focus of Lesson: To help students begin to understand the morphology or meaningful language units within words and to use this knowledge to build new words.

Whole-Class Instruction: Set up a large pocket chart, partitioned into three sections, with the following headings: "Prefixes," "Base Words," and "Suffixes." Fill the chart with index cards displaying several familiar base words, such as *play*, *do*, and *look*. Invite children to come up front to sit around the chart, and explain that adding prefixes or suffixes (*un-*, *re-*, *-ing*, *-er*) to common words changes the meaning of these words.

Following the whole class mini-lesson, use Reader's Workshop time to have children look for examples of base words with prefixes and/or suffixes in their reading books. Ask them to use sticky notes to mark the pages where they find these examples, and to record the words they find. During the group share portion of the Readers' Workshop, list the children's discoveries on a class chart and display the chart in the classroom as a reference tool.

Prefixes	Base Words		Suffixes		
	play	+	ing	=	playing
re +	play	=			replay
	play	+	er	=	player

WORDS OF NOTE

"Words that share the same roots belong, in general, to the same meaning 'family' and are related to one another. Not only is an awareness of this fact useful to vocabulary development, it can help with students' learning spelling as well...an awareness of the spelling-meaning connection can become a strategy students can use when they are uncertain about the spelling of a word. We tell the students, 'Try to think of a word that is related in meaning and in spelling to the one you're trying to spell; such a word may provide the needed clue.'"

—Dr. Shane Templeton,
University of Nevada, Reno

Mini-Lesson #4

Essential Understanding: *"What else do good spellers use to build words?"*

"They use five important spelling rules to build new words:
  They always put a u after q.
  They know that every syllable has a vowel or y.
They know that the silent e drops when adding endings that begin with a vowel.
They double consonants at the ends of some words before adding an ending that begins with a vowel.
They change y to i when adding the endings -er, -est, -ed, or -s (-es)."

Focus of Lesson: The intent of this lesson is to introduce children to the five important spelling rules, to share these rules, and then to ask students to look for examples to verify them.

Whole-Class Instruction (for the first two rules): Prepare a large chart listing all five important spelling rules (see above). Mask each rule until it has been discussed or directly taught during one of the following mini-lessons.

Mrs. H.: There are five important spelling rules that good spellers use. I am going to share two of these rules today with you.

(Mrs. H. uncovers the first of the five rules written on the chart paper.)

Mrs. H.: The first rule states that the letter *q* is always followed by the letter *u* in words. Who can think of a word that begins with the letter *q*?

Jason: The word *queen* starts with the letter *q*.

Mrs. H.: Yes, Jason. Do you know how to spell the word queen?

Jason: Q—u—e—e—n

Mrs. H.: Does this word confirm the rule?

(The children nod in agreement.)

(Mrs. H. then invites the children to return to their tables and to work cooperatively to search through alphabet books and dictionaries for words beginning with the letter q. *The children list their discoveries on large pieces of chart paper, as shown to the right.)*

(Mrs. H. then shares the enlarged chart at right with the class.)

Mrs. H.: Our second rule for today states that every syllable in a word must have a vowel or *y*. Who can recite the names of the vowels aloud?

Brett: They're *a, e, i, o, u,* and sometimes *y*.

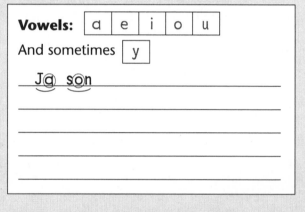

Mrs. H.: Yes, Brett. Those are the vowels that act like cement to hold the consonants in words together. Let's pretend we're word detectives for a few minutes. Let's try this rule out with our names. Let's clap the syllables in our names as we write them on our chart.

(Mrs. H. says aloud, Ja—son, as the children clap twice. She then writes the name on the chart.)

Mrs. H.: Jason, is there a vowel in each part or syllable of your name?

Jason: Yes, there's an *a* in the first part and an *o* in the second part.

(Mrs. H. confirms the rule with three or four additional children's names and writes those on the chart.)

Whole-Class Instruction (for the third rule): A few days later, uncover the third spelling rule for the class to check out and verify.

SAMPLE DIALOGUE:

Mrs. H.: There's another important rule that good spellers need to know: We drop the silent *e* from a word when we add endings that begin with a vowel. To see an example, let's read the popular rhyme "It's Raining, It's Pouring," together.

> **IT'S RAINING, IT'S POURING**
>
> It's raining, it's pouring,
> The old man is snoring.
>
> He bumped his head
> When he went to bed
> And he couldn't get up
> In the morning.
>
> —Traditional

(Mrs. H. writes the word snore *on the chalkboard and directs the children's attention back to the poem.)*

Mrs. H.: How did the word *snore* change when the poet wrote *snoring*?

Lori: The word lost its silent *e*.

Mrs. H.: Yes. Let's try this rule with the following words that end with a silent *e*.

(Mrs. H. writes the words bake, hope, *and* like *on the chalkboard.)*

Mrs. H.: Who would like to change the word *bake* to *baking*?

Jason: I can erase the *e* and add *-ing*.

(Jason proceeds to the chalkboard and writes b—a—k—i—n—g.*)*

Mrs. H.: Great. Now please try changing the words *hope* and *like* to *hoping* and *liking* using the new rule. Please add these words to your personal dictionaries.

Whole-Class Instruction (for the fourth and fifth rules): You can teach the remaining two rules to students in much the same way. As shown at right, action words are great examples to use for the fourth rule (doubling consonants at the end of words before adding an ending that begins with a vowel).

At right are examples of words to use to teach the final rule: change *y* to *i* when adding the endings *-er*, *-est*, *-ed*, or *-s* (*-es*).

By the conclusion of these mini-lessons, all five spelling rules—with examples—should be unmasked and displayed on the rules chart in the classroom. We also recommend having children add examples of these important rules to their personal spelling dictionaries.

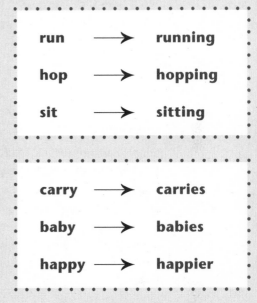

Mini-Lesson #5

Essential Understanding: *"How else do good spellers edit their writing?"*

"Good spellers refer to classroom spelling charts and personal spelling dictionaries, which list common prefixes, suffixes and important spelling rules."

Focus of Lesson: These mini-lessons focus on facilitating students' application of additional spelling strategies. Students use known visual patterns and/or meaning units (morphemes) as well as important spelling rules to edit their own writing.

Whole-Class Instruction: As with other editing mini-lessons, these mini-lessons are most effectively taught as part of Writers' Workshop sessions. Select an anonymous student piece of writing or create your own sample with spelling errors that ignore the important rules. Using an overhead projector, share the unedited piece with your students and invite them to fix the spelling errors.

SAMPLE DIALOGUE:

Mrs. H.: Before we can publish this story, we need to edit for spelling errors. What errors can you find?

Elise: The word *loving* is spelled incorrectly. One important spelling rule on our chart says that the silent *e* drops when adding endings that begin with a vowel. The word *love* ends in a silent *e* and the suffix -*ing* begins with a vowel.

Mrs. H.: Elise, please come up and correct the misspelling.

(Elise crosses out the incorrect spelling and writes loving *above the misspelled word.)*

(Mrs. H continues the lesson, working her way through the misspelled words, each time explicitly encouraging her students to use classroom spelling charts and personal spelling dictionaries to aid their editing process.)

SAMPLE DRAFT

The <u>loveing</u> <u>qeen</u> lived with her kind husband in a big <u>castl</u> in the <u>foot hills</u> of England. They were the <u>happyest</u> royal couple in all the land, until one day a jealous sorcerer snuck into their home and cast an evil spell on the unsuspecting <u>coupl</u>. As the evil sorcerer was <u>runing</u> away from the castle, he <u>triped</u> over a large rock and fell unconscious to the ground.

Spelling Rules-Based Editing Corrections:

love—loving	castle	happiest	running
queen	foothills	couple	tripped

TEACHER'S CORNER

Too often visual aides in a classroom run the risk of seeming like "background décor" or wallpaper, rather than useful reference tools. It is imperative at this stage that teachers make expectations very clear about students' independent use of these valuable word study tools.

Guided Practice Activities

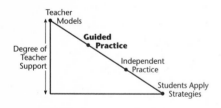

In this section, we offer seven guided practice activities. As in the previous two chapters, each activity or pair of activities accompanies a mini-lesson from the preceding section and helps students put into action what they have just learned in the lesson. These guided practice activities are interactive experiences that enable children to learn how to build new words. They can be used for whole-class or small-group lessons. The chart on page 85 provides an overview of the scope of these activities, their purpose, and the lessons they are intended to accompany.

Overview of Guided Practice Activities for Phase Three

Guided Practice Activity	Use For	Accompanies This Mini-Lesson
Pattern Sheets for Building on Known Words	Building on and expanding core of known words	What do good spellers do to build new words?
Discovering Parts of Compound Words	Joining known words to form compound words	How else do good spellers build new words?
Pattern Sheets for Adding Suffixes and Prefixes to Known Words	Adding endings (and beginnings) to words	What else do good spellers do to build new words?
Read Around the Room for Spelling Rule 1 Read Around the Room for Spelling Rule 2 Read Around the Room for Spelling Rules 3, 4, and 5	Using important spelling rules to build new words	What is something else good spellers use to build words?
Reference Tools	Editing	How else do good spellers edit their writing?

Guided Practice Activity:
PATTERN SHEETS FOR BUILDING ON KNOWN WORDS

Purpose: To use visual and auditory features of known words to build new words

Use for: Building on and expanding core of known words

Materials and Preparation: Pattern sheets; easel; marker. Select the words that your students need to practice. Prepare a wordpattern sheet (see page 86) by filling in the top section with the desired words. Have available sufficient photocopies of the sheet for each member of the class.

Procedure: Gather the children in front of the easel to demonstrate this word-building strategy.

SAMPLE DIALOGUE:

Mrs. M.: Good spellers use their eyes, ears, and mouths to build on words that they already know to write new words. Today we are going to try making new words from some words that we already know how to spell. Look at the easel.

I'm going to write a word that we've been practicing.

(Mrs. M. writes the word me *on the easel.)*

Does anyone recognize this word?

Renata: I do.

Andrew: I do, too.

Noah: It's *me*.

Mrs. M.: Yes, it is. Now if I know the word *me*, then how would I write the word *he*?

Peter: Write an *h* instead of the *m*.

Mrs. M.: Yes, that's right! We would change the *m* to an *h*.

(Mrs. M. writes the word he *on the easel.)*

Mrs. M.: If we know *me* and *he*, then how would we write *she*?

Shelley: Put an *sh*, just like in my name.

(Mrs. M. writes the word she *on the easel.)*

Mrs. M.: Great! And how about *be*?

Helen: Put a *b*.

(Mrs. M. writes the word be *on the easel.)*

Mrs. M.: What great builders all of you are! All of the words that we just built are on this sheet that I'm going to give to each of you. When you get one, you can go back to your seat and get out a pencil, scissors, and a glue stick.

(Mrs. M. distributes the reproducible sheets to each child.)

Mrs. M.: Now let's take a look at our sheet. Take your reading finger and let's read all the words that we made.

Class: *Me, he, she,* and *be*.

Mrs. M.: Great reading! Now let's take our pencils and trace those words. Let's say each word as we write them in the spaces. Finally, we are going to cut out the letters on the back of the page and build the words *me, he, she,* and *be* and glue them in the empty space.

Children write and say the words on the first sheet and then build new words. On the second sheet they cut out the letters and build the words in the space provided.

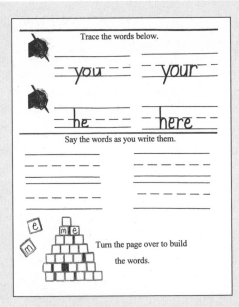

(Mrs. M. walks around the room guiding the children through each of these steps.)

Words to use for reproducible pattern sheets:

no - go	zoo - boo	dad - did	has - had
go- got	bus - but	of - off	let - get
in - into	out - our	on - one	eat - ear
is - his	the - they	he - here	come - came
up - us	them - there	you - your	some - same
to - do	then - when	can - an	
of - if	there - where	this - that	

Guided Practice Activity: DISCOVERING PARTS OF COMPOUND WORDS

Purpose: Building new words from two known words

Use for: Joining known words to form compound words

Materials: Easel; poem written on chart paper; markers; a copy of the poem "Bugs" for each child (see page 88); a blank copy of the compound word parts sheet (see page 88)

Procedure: Write the poem "Bugs" by Meish Goldish on chart paper and photocopy the poem for each child. Gather the children around the easel to share the poem.

SAMPLE DIALOGUE:

Mrs. M.: Today we're going to read a poem called "Bugs." Your job is to see if you can find some compound words hidden in the poem.

(Mrs. M. reads the poem to the class. As the children identify the compound words in the poem, Mrs. M. or a child comes up to the easel and uses a slash mark to indicate the breaks between the

BUGS

June Bug, stink bug,
Lady/bug, cinch bug,
Water bug, pink bug,
Please-don't-pinch bug!

Horse/fly, house/fly,
Dragon/fly, deer fly,
Fire/fly, fruit fly,
Buzzing-in-your-ear fly!

Honey/bee, bumble/bee,
Queen bee, drone bee,
Worker bee, nurse bee,
Leave-me-alone bee!

Gypsy moth, luna moth,
Beetle and mosquito.
Bugs and insects
Really are neat-o!

Cock/roach, katy/did,
Cricket and cicada.
Grass/hopper, mantis,
Catch you all later!

—By Miesh Goldish, *Thematic Poems, Songs, and Fingerplays*, Scholastic Inc.

two words in each compound word. When this whole-class activity is completed, each child gets his/her own copy of the poem. Mrs. M. asks them to locate the compound words and separate them on the sheet, also using a slash mark. Next the children fill in the lines on the compound word parts reproducible; this gives them practice writing both the word parts and the whole compound words they found.)

Compound Word Parts

lady	+	bug	=	ladybug
horse	+	fly	=	horsefly
house	+	fly	=	housefly
dragon	+	fly	=	dragonfly
fire	+	fly	=	firefly
honey	+	bee	=	honeybee
bumble	+	bee	=	bumblebee
cock	+	roach	=	cockroach
katy	+	did	=	katydid
grass	+	hopper	=	grasshopper

Guided Practice Activity: PATTERN SHEETS FOR ADDING SUFFIXES AND PREFIXES TO KNOWN WORDS

Purpose: Building new words by adding endings

Use for: Adding endings (and beginnings) to words

Materials and Preparation: Pattern sheets (see page 89) for each child; easel; marker; chart paper. Have available a copy of the pattern sheets for every child. Make a template of these pattern sheets on chart paper.

Procedure: Gather the children at the easel first for a demonstration of the following strategy.

SAMPLE DIALOGUE:

Mrs. M.: Today we are going to add some endings to words that we already know to make some new words.

(Mrs. M. writes the word look *on the easel.)*

Tracey: You wrote *look*.

Mrs. M.: Yes, that's right. But now I want to make some new words from the word *look*. What if I wanted to write *looks*?

Spelling Success in the Early Grades • Scholastic Teaching Resources

Gina: Add an *s* at the end.

Mrs. M.: How about if I wanted to write the sentence, "He looked at the shoes." How would I write *looked*?

Eileen: Add an *-ed* at the end of *look*.

Mrs. M.: What if I wanted to write *looking* in my sentence: "I am looking at some books"?

Bill: Add *-ing* to *look*.

Mrs. M.: Super building! Let's read all the words we made from the word *look*.

Class: *Look, looks, looked, looking.*

Mrs. M.: Now each of you is going to take one of these sheets and try adding endings to some other words. Be sure to write the entire new word on each line, not just the ending.

(Mrs. M. walks around the room helping the children.)

(When the children have finished work on the sheets, Mrs. M. gathers them back at the easel to discuss the new words that they built. She then fills in the words on the chart paper.)

> ## Adding Endings to Words
> ### S   ed   ing
> Add the endings to the words below.
>
> **look** _____ _____ _____
>
> **play** _____ _____ _____
>
> **walk** _____ _____ _____
>
> **yell** _____ _____ _____

Extension: Follow the same procedure for adding prefixes and other suffixes to common base or root words. (Additional pattern sheets are on page 102.)

Guided Practice Activity:
READ AROUND THE ROOM FOR SPELLING RULE 1

Purpose: To use important spelling rules to build new words

Use for: Remembering to put a *u* after the letter *q*

Materials: Alphabet books; class charts; alphabet charts; personal dictionaries; easel; marker; chart paper; piece of paper for each child

Procedure: Gather the children and tell them that they are going to "read around the room" in a search for words that begin with the letter *q*. Explain that reading around the room means that they can look for this information anywhere in the classroom. All of the following might be sources:

- Personal dictionaries
- Alphabet books
- Alphabet charts
- Class charts
- Bulletin boards
- Reading books
- Poetry books

Tell the children that when they find a word that begins with the letter *q*, they should write it down on their papers. Allot them approximately 15–20 minutes, and then invite them back to the easel to share their findings. List the words on chart paper.

SAMPLE DIALOGUE:

Mrs. M.: I can tell you did a lot of reading around the room. What did you notice about words that begin with the letter *q*?

Jerry: They all have a *u* after the *q*.

Mrs. M.: That's right! Whenever you have a word that begins with the letter *q*, it always has a *u* that follows. Let's add this rule to our Spelling Rules chart and hang it in the writing center for us to refer to when we write.

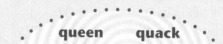

queen	quack
quilt	quarter
quick	quiz
quiet	quit

Guided Practice Activity:
READ AROUND THE ROOM FOR SPELLING RULE 2

Purpose: To use important spelling rules to build new words

Use for: Knowing that every syllable of a word has a vowel or a *y*

Materials and Preparation: Vowel sheet for every child (see below); easel; chart paper; marker. Make a photocopy of the vowel sheet for every child. Also make a template of this sheet on chart paper.

Procedure: Gather the children around the easel for a demonstration.

SAMPLE DIALOGUE:

Mrs. M.: Today we're going to talk about another spelling rule that we can add to our Spelling Rules chart in our writing corner. But before we can do that, we must see for ourselves if this rule is true. The rule is about vowels. Who remembers which letters are vowels?

Patricia: *a, e, i, o, u*

Andrew: And sometimes *y*.

Mrs. M.: That's right! Let's sing our vowel song.

(Mrs. M. focuses the children's attention on the vowel song hanging in the poetry center. The class sings it as a reminder.)

Mrs. M.: You said that *a, e, i, o, u* and sometimes *y* are our vowels, so I am going to write these letters in my boxes—one letter in each box.

(Mrs. M. does just this on her template on chart paper.)

Mrs. M.: Our rule, which we have to prove is true before we add it to our spelling rules chart, is that every syllable of every word that we write has a vowel in it. I'm going to give

a	e	i	o	u

y

Sarah	go
yes	Andrew
me	stop
you	to

Vowel Sheet (*Example*)

each of you one of these sheets. The first thing that I would like you to do is write the vowels in the boxes as I just did, and then take some time to write words on the lines underneath. Write only words that you absolutely, positively know are spelled correctly. They can be sight words, friends' names, names of your brothers and sisters—any words, as long as you know how to write them. I'm setting my timer for 15 minutes. When the bell rings, we'll meet back at the easel.

Mrs. M.: *(as the bell rings)* Time's up. Come and join me. Let's take a look at what you found.

(Mrs. M. invites the children up to the easel to write the words that they brainstormed. Together, Mrs. M. and the children identify the vowel in each syllable of every word.)

TEACHER'S CORNER

The song *Vowels*, sung to the tune of "Bingo," makes a wonderful addition to any print-rich classroom. If you print out this song on chart paper and mount it on a classroom wall, you will have a great resource when introducing this activity.

VOWELS (sung to "Bingo")

There are all those words that have special letters and <u>vowels</u> are their names – oh!

A-e-i-o-u, a-e-i-o-u, a-e-i-o-u, and <u>vowels</u> are their names-oh!

(Now have the children repeat the song, leaving out the first letter, a, and clapping once instead:)

Clap-e-i-o-u, clap-e-i-o-u, clap-e-i-o-u and <u>vowels</u> are their names-oh!

(Repeat the song four more times, each time leaving out the next vowel letter and making a clap sound instead. The final verse will look like this:)

There are all those words that have special letters and <u>vowels</u> are their names – oh!

Clap-clap-clap-clap-clap, *(repeat two more times)*, and <u>vowels</u> are their names—oh!

A fun alternative for this song is to use finger-spelling (based on the alphabet on page 42) instead of claps for each vowel letter.

Guided Practice Activity:
READ AROUND THE ROOM FOR SPELLING RULES 3, 4, AND 5

Purpose: To use important spelling rules to build new words.

Used for: Knowing how to:
Drop the silent *e* when adding endings that begin with a vowel
Double consonants at the end of words before adding an ending that begins with a vowel
Change *y* to *i* when adding the endings -*er*, -*est*, -*ed*, or -*s* (-*es*).

Materials and Preparation: Pattern sheet; easel; chart paper; marker. Print the above spelling rules on chart paper. Have available a pattern sheet (see page 92) for each child.

Procedure: Gather the children at the easel for a demonstration of these strategies.

SAMPLE DIALOGUE:

Mrs. M.: Today we are going to review some of our spelling rules. *(Mrs. M. and the children read the rules together.)* Let's take another look at our first rule: Drop the silent *e* when adding endings that begin with a vowel. I have the word care written on my chart paper. How would I write *caring*?

Andrew: *c-a-r-i-n-g*

(Mrs. M demonstrates rules 4 and 5 in the same manner. For each, she reviews the rule, shows an example, and adds an ending.)

Mrs. M.: Now you are going to practice these rules on your own. Each of you will get your own sheet. Your job is to add endings to the words on the sheet. We'll meet back at the easel in about 15 minutes when the timer goes off for a group share.

Name_____

Spelling Rule: Drop the silent *e* when adding endings that begin with a vowel.

share _____

make _____

hope _____

love _____

Spelling Rule: Double consonants at the end of words before adding and ending that begins with a vowel.

stop _____

pop _____

hit _____

stir _____

Spelling Rule: Change *y* to *i* when adding the endings *-er*, *-est*, *-ed*, and *-s* (*-es*).

worry _____

busy _____

try _____

family _____

Guided Practice Activity: REFERENCE TOOLS

Purpose: To use reference tools such as spelling charts, spelling rules, and common endings to edit writing

Use for: Editing

Materials: "Silly Story;" spelling charts; spelling rules; common endings chart; easel; chart paper; marker. Make photocopies of "Silly Story" (see page 93) for each child. Copy the story on chart paper or make a transparency for the overhead projector.

Procedure: Gather the children and review the spelling rules with them. Tell students that all these rules have been broken in the story you are about to give them. Distribute a copy of the Silly Story to each child. We recommend using a "jigsaw" small-group arrangement for this activity. Divide the children into five groups and assign each group one spelling rule. Each group is responsible for fixing the part of the story that broke their assigned rule. Choose one member of each group to act as recorder. After the group as a whole has made a decision, the recorder uses white correction tape to cover up the errors and fix them on one photocopy of the story.

When the groups have finished their work, gather everyone around the easel or the overhead. Ask one

> **TEACHER'S CORNER**
> Have your Spelling Rules chart visible for children to refer to during this activity. It is also helpful to have a photocopy of the rules for each child to keep in his or her writing folder.

child (the recorder or another student) from each group to explain or demonstrate how to fix the errors that his or her group was responsible for finding.

> ### Silly Story: <u>The Qeens Tale</u>
>
> The qeen sat qietly in her room knitting her qilt. Suddnly she realized that she ran out of yarn. She went in her closet to get more, but she didn't have any. She needed to go to the store. She tried rideing her bicycle, but her tires were flat. She tried useing the phone to call a cab, but the phone didn't work. So she took the bus. The bus kept stoping to pick up lots of people. She finlly got to the store. She found the yarn she needed. She bought it and carryed it all the way home.

This boy is checking the Spelling Rules chart he keeps in his folder as he helps his group fix part of the "Silly Story."

Independent Practice: Learning Center Activities

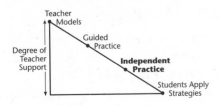

As in Phase One and Phase Two, we follow up mini-lessons and guided practice in Phase Three with an opportunity for students to explore a range of hands-on activities. The independent activities for this phase reinforce building words using the visual and auditory features of known words. Each activity includes a period of modeling and instruction—essentially, an

Overview of Independent Practice Activities for Phase Three

Independent Practice Activity	Learning Style Connection	Purpose
Building New Words	Linguistic and Interpersonal	Good spellers build on and expand their core of known words.
Compound Word Puzzles	Linguistic and Spatial	Good spellers join known words to make compound words.
Changing the Meaning of Known Root Words by Adding Prefixes and Suffixes	Linguistic and Spatial	Good spellers add prefixes and suffixes to known words to change the meaning of the root words.
Spelling Rule Games	Linguistic, Spatial, and Interpersonal	Good spellers use important spelling rules to build new words.
Becoming Good Editors	Linguistic and Interpersonal	Good spellers use spelling charts (i.e., tricky parts, common beginnings and endings), personal dictionaries, and print around the room to check the spelling of words.

introduction to the activity. After this introduction, place the activity into a learning center and make it available to the class. It is here that the independent learning takes place. As in Chapters 2 and 3, the activities are balanced to take into account the different learning styles that young children bring to the classroom.

Independent Practice Activity: BUILDING NEW WORDS

Learning Style: Linguistic and Interpersonal

Purpose: Good spellers build on and expand their core of known words

Materials and Preparation: 3" x 5" index cards; magnetic letters; shaving cream; colored sand in tub. For each of three center groups, prepare a set of 3" x 5" index cards with core words on one side and expanded words on other side. (See example below.) Use words such as: *of-off, he-she, then-when, there-where* and *he-him.*

Modeling and Introduction: Invite the children to the rug circle. Remind them of how they used the pattern sheets in the guided practice lesson to build on and expand sight words they already know.

of	off

SAMPLE DIALOGUE:

Ms. K.: Today we will practice building new words in our word study centers. I'll give each center a set of cards like this. *(She holds up an index card with* of *written on one side.)* Paul, would you be my partner and build the word *of* using the magnetic letters on the white board?

Paul: Yes, I can do that!

(When Paul does this correctly, Ms. K. asks if he can make of *into* off, *again using the magnetic letters that she has set up on the white board. Paul correctly adds the* f *to the end, and Ms. K. turns the index card to the other side and shows the class that Paul has changed the word correctly to make a new word.)*

Learning Center Activity: Tell the children they will work with a partner to build new words, asking 6–8 children to gather at each of three center tables. Explain that students in each pair are to take turns choosing an index card. Have one partner build and change the sight word; then together the partners check the change by looking at the word on the other side of the card. Have one group use magnetic letters to build new words. The other two groups use shaving cream and colored sand. Review with students the rules for cooperating and working quietly with a partner. (These rules might be posted in the room for all to see.) Walk around the room, making sure that each group is working together to check and correct the expanded and changed words. When you feel that they can work independently on this activity, stand to the side and just observe.

Extension Activity: Offer an extended version of this activity at learning centers on another day. Ask children to use the word wall to find sight words that they can expand or change by adding phonemes.

94

Independent Practice Activity: COMPOUND WORD PUZZLES: JOINING KNOWN WORDS TO FORM COMPOUND WORDS

Learning Style: Linguistic and Spatial

Purpose: Good spellers build new words by joining known sight words to form compound words.

Materials and Preparation: 8" x 10" card stock or 4" x 6" index cards; extra paper; markers; crayons. Prepare at least 10 sets of compound sight word puzzle mats for each center (6 to 8 students). You can make puzzle mats by writing compound words on 8" x 10" card stock paper or 4" x 6" index cards and laminating them. (See example below.) Cut the paper or card in half to form the two parts of the word puzzle. (Alternately, blank commercial puzzles can be purchased from school supply catalogues or from teacher stores.)

Modeling and Introduction: Gather the children together on the class rug and remind them that they learned to identify compound words in poems during the guided practice lesson. Tell them, "Today we will practice building compound words in our activity centers." To introduce the activity, invite one of the children to be your partner. On the rug, spread out three of the word puzzle mats of prepared compound words. Invite your partner to make a compound word by matching two of the words on the puzzle pieces. Continue this process until there are three sets of matched compound words.

Learning Center Activity: Divide the class into centers and place 10 sets of mixed-up puzzle pieces in the middle of each center table. Have the children in each group take turns finding the matching compound words and putting them together. Circulate among the tables until you feel sure that students understand the activity and are working well independently. When the children have finished building the sets of compound words, they draw pictures to illustrate the word pairs.

Extension Activity: You can offer two alternate versions of this activity at learning centers on other days. In one activity, have students make their own word puzzles by writing compound words on card stock and cutting them apart for other children to put together. For the other activity, you'll need to prepare ahead of time special cards by folding square pieces of paper into thirds. On the outside of the two end flaps, write the two parts of the compound word. Leave the center inside piece blank for the student to write the whole word.

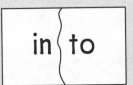

Independent Practice Activity:
ADDING BEGINNINGS AND ENDINGS: CHANGING THE MEANING OF KNOWN ROOT WORDS BY ADDING PREFIXES AND SUFFIXES

Learning Style: Linguistic and Spatial

Purpose: Good spellers add prefixes and suffixes to known words to change the meaning of the root words.

Materials and Preparation: Stock card paper or 4" x 6" index cards; magnetic letters. Prepare these cards following same directions as for compound word cards (see page 95) but cut the cards into rectangles, not puzzle pieces. For this activity, write common prefixes written on one set of cards, suffixes on another, and known root words on a third set. Prepare about ten sets of cards for each center.

Modeling and Introduction: Remind children of what they learned during recent mini-lessons and guided practice activities: how to identify and build new words by adding beginnings (prefixes) and endings (suffixes) to known root words.

SAMPLE DIALOGUE:

(Ms. K. shows the children the sets of word cards with the different prefixes, suffixes, and root words written on them. She holds up the card with play on it.)

Ms K.: Who can build a new word using a suffix or a prefix?

Josh : *(raising his hand)* I can put the card with -*ing* at the end of *play* and make *playing*.

Michelle: I can add *re-* to the front of *playing* and make it into *replaying*.

Josh: Replaying means you are playing the game again!

(Ms. K. tells students that they will now work at centers to see how many new words they can make by using the cards with the beginnings (prefixes), endings (suffixes), and root words written on them.)

Cards

re

play

ing

re	play	ing

Learning Center Activity: For this activity, set up center tables with word cards. Place the sets of word cards in mixed-up piles in the center of each table. Provide instructions at the centers telling children to take turns building new words using the root words, prefixes, and suffixes; saying the new word; and showing the meaning by using the word in a sentence. In addition, you can provide paper and crayons at each center so children can illustrate the meaning of some of the new words.

Variation: Use puzzle-shaped cards for prefixes, suffixes, and root words and have students build new words as they do in the activity on page 95.

Independent Practice Activity: SPELLING RULE GAMES

Learning Style: Linguistic, Spatial, and Interpersonal

Purpose: To reinforce that good spellers use important spelling rules to build new words:

1. They always put *u* after *q*.
2. They know that every syllable has a vowel or *y*.
3. They know that the silent *e* drops when adding endings that begin with a vowel.
4. They double the consonants at the end of some words before adding an ending that begins with a vowel.
5. They change *y* to *i* when adding the endings *-er*, *-est*, *-ed*, or *-s (-es)*.

Materials and Preparation: A different set of materials at each of five centers:

1. Puzzle pieces on card stock or index cards with the *qu* words written on them; crayons and paper for illustrating the *qu* words the group has made
2. Vowel sheets for writing words; pencils and markers for circling vowels; class book sets for finding words
3. Magnetic letters; magnetic blackboards or white boards; white board markers and erasers for each pair of partners; cards with known words that end with silent *e* such as *ride, hide, slide*, etc.
4. Word letter cubes or shaving cream; cards with sight words from the word wall such as *run, hop, flop*, etc.
5. Shaving cream or colored sand in a large tub

Modeling and Introduction: Remind the children that they learned important spelling rules as they played "read around the room" during the guided practice lesson. Explain that they will work in five word study centers, and that each center will practice changing words using one of the five spelling rules. Point to the rules, displayed on a class chart, and review them with children, asking them to come up with examples. Have a copy of one rule at each of the five independent learning centers. With one child as a partner, demonstrate and model the center activities. When you feel that they understand the activities, break them into five groups and assemble the groups at the five learning center tables, where they will each work with a partner.

Learning Center Activities:

Table 1: The children take turns putting together the *qu* puzzle words and then drawing pictures to illustrate the new words.

Table 2: The children work in pairs to find and write down as many words as they can from the class reading books on their table. Then they use their markers to circle the vowels in each of those words. (See sample vowel sheet, page 90.)

Table 3: Word cards with silent *e* are in the middle of the table. One partner picks a card with a silent *e*. The other partner uses magnetic letters or the white boards and markers to build the word and then, applying the rule, adds an ending such as *-ing* or *-er* to the root word. Partners take turns.

Table 4: Word cards with words ending in consonants are in the center of the table. The children take turns writing the word in their pond of shaving cream (or building the words with letter cubes) and then (applying the rule), they add the ending.

Table 5: Word cards with words that end with *y* (*happy, easy, funny, silly,* etc.) are in the center of the table. The children take turns writing the words (in their shaving cream pond or sand) and then (applying the rule), they add the endings *-est, -ed, er,* or *-s* (*-es*).

Extension Activity: Children can use appropriate words from the word wall for any of these activities.

Independent Practice Activity: BECOMING GOOD EDITORS

Learning Style: Linguistic and Interpersonal

Purpose: Good spellers use classroom word walls, spelling charts (i.e., spelling rules, tricky parts, common beginnings and endings), personal dictionaries, and print around the room to check the spelling of words.

Materials: Copies of student journal writing—students may volunteer their journals or Writer's Workshop story drafts (make sure there are sufficient written drafts for each pair of students, plus extra material if the students finish their editing piece); yellow highlighting markers, "boo-boo" tape (wide white correction tape), and pencils for each center

Modeling and Introduction: Remind the children of how they used the rules for building new words to edit a piece of writing during the guided instruction lesson.

SAMPLE DIALOGUE:

Ms. K: Today you will work with a partner to edit a piece of journal writing or a piece of writing from Writer's Workshop. You can use your personal dictionaries to help you.

Sam: We can also use the words around the room and the charts with the rules that we know.

Andrew: And the word wall!

Ms. K.: Excellent remembering! Yes, all of those references will help you.

(She divides the class into five groups and asks children with each group to pair up into partners. She gives each pair a writing sample to work on together. As the children work independently, Ms. K. circulates, answering questions and helping students stay on task. Later, during the sharing circle, the children share some of the rules they used to make corrections. Ms. K. writes them down on a chart for the class.)

Assessment of Student Learning

As children progress through Phase Three of word study lessons and spelling activities, continue to make reflective kid watching an instructional priority. Data collected from everyday learning settings and from classroom-based assessments are essential for making informed instructional decisions.

ONGOING ASSESSMENT

Continue to use your log to record observations of your students during guided practice and independent learning center activities. For Phase Three, as for the previous two phases, these observations provide a rich source of information as they highlight students' successes and confusions.

Observations Log

For Phase Three, use your observations log to ascertain how students are utilizing known words to make new words. On a daily basis, you might choose to observe a different small group of students. This will allow you to focus on the selected children, while remaining accessible to the rest of the class. When reviewing the work or task at hand, it's helpful to highlight a child's application of one or two strategies. We recommended that you use the log below, or one similar to it, to record observations about students' ability to build new words during independent practice activities and/or journal writing. In the example below, the teacher seeks evidence of the spelling rules involved in building new words.

Name	Date	Observations
Eileen		
Debbie		
Gina		
Pam	6/24/02	use of appropriate inflectional endings (-ing, -s)

As you make your observations for this phase, some focusing questions to ask yourself include:

⊙ Can the child add, delete, and/or substitute letters within words to build words?

⊙ Can the child combine known high-frequency words to form compound words?

⊙ Can the child use known parts of words (morphemes) to spell more complex, multi-syllabic words?

⊙ Can the child add familiar prefixes to common base words?

⊙ Can the child add familiar suffixes to common base words?

⊙ Is the child implementing spelling rules to build new words?

SPECIFIC CLASSROOM-BASED ASSESSMENTS

The following three specific classroom-based assessment tools will again provide you with instructionally useful information:

- **Building New Words Assessment:** Administer this assessment in small or large groups. Read directions and, if necessary, give an example for each substitution or addition. This assessment addresses students' understanding of utilizing the visual and auditory features of known words to build new words.

- **Contextual Dictation:** Dictate 3–5 sentences that include words representing Phase Three strategies—for instance, addition of prefixes, suffixes, and evidence of use of spelling rules.

- **Student Writing Sample:** Select a writing sample from a student's journal to assess the student's understanding of visual and auditory features of words.

Building New Words Assessment

The following student assessment should help you evaluate a child's progress in adding, deleting, and/or substituting letters of known words to build new words. To administer it, read the directions aloud and, if necessary, give an example for each substitution or addition. This more formal assessment tool can be used in addition to journal writing samples when you seek evidence of the spelling rules involved in building new words.

Name: _____   Date: _____

1. Make four new words by changing the beginning sound in the word *cat*.

   _____ _____ _____ _____

2. Make four new words by changing the ending sound in the word *big*.

   _____ _____ _____ _____

3. Make four new words by combining the following words: *cup + cake, sun + tan, class + room, in + side.*

   _____ _____ _____ _____

4. Make four new words by adding the prefix *un-* to *do, happy, tie,* and *fair*.

   _____ _____ _____ _____

5. Make four new words by adding the ending (suffix) *–ing* to *play, work, eat,* and *jump*.

   _____ _____ _____ _____

6. Make four new words by adding the ending *-ing* to *win, run, hit,* and *jog*.

   _____ _____ _____ _____

Contextual Dictation

Dictate the following three short sentences to seek evidence of students' application of important Phase Three strategies:

1. The king was running and bumped into the queen. *(evidence of spelling rules)*

2. The boy was unhappy about having to redo his work. *(evidence of adding prefixes)*

3. The ballplayer had a deep suntan. *(evidence of compound words)*

Student Writing Sample

Select writing samples from students' journals to specifically assess their independent application of Phase Three word-building strategies. A sample student journal sample entry follows:

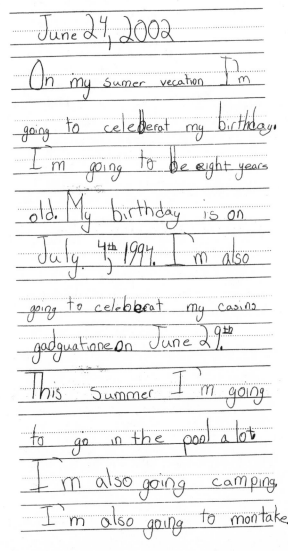

Teacher's analysis: After reviewing this sample, Mrs. Varrone documented the use of appropriate endings in the child's writing—*going, camping, years,* and of the correct spelling of the compound word *birthday.*

Important Endings
er

List names you know that end
with -er.

_____

_____

_____

_____

How many other words can you
think of that end in -er?

_____

_____

_____

Important Endings
y

List friends' names that end in y.

_____

_____

_____

_____

How many other words can you
think of that end in y?

_____

_____

_____

_____

Spelling Success in the Early Grades • Scholastic Teaching Resources

CHAPTER 5

Making Connections: Using Common Word Families (Phonograms or Rimes)

PHASE FOUR: APRIL–JUNE

In the final phase of our spelling/word study approach, students are introduced to the most common phonograms, which will extend their spelling vocabulary. The lessons and activities for Phase Four target selected phonograms from the list of 38 common phonograms ranked by researcher Edward Fry (Fry, 1998).

During Shared Reading sessions, you can read aloud various poems featuring the targeted word families or phonograms and use these as the basis for mini-lessons and activities. On page 104 are listed some of our favorite poems, traditional rhymes, and rhyming texts.

Following a Shared Reading of a poem or rhyming text, distribute copies of the text for the children to store in their poetry folders. Invite students to circle words containing the common phonograms (e.g., *Jill, hill*; *wall, fall*). We often notice that after several Shared

Reading lessons, children comment that they have discovered additional examples of words containing these targeted word families in their independent reading books.

You might also invite the class to create "Environmental Print Word Family Collages." These are 3-dimensional wall displays featuring real-world products, signs, and logos that feature the common phonograms. This activity will also successfully heighten your students' awareness of the common word families that are hidden in the environmental print that they read everyday. The poster at right provides an example.

Targeted Phonogram	Rhyme, Poem, or Rhyming Text
ay	"Down by the Bay" (Raffi; traditional song)
ill	Jack and Jill (nursery rhyme)
all	Humpty Dumpty (nursery rhyme)
at	*The Cat in the Hat* by Dr. Seuss
ing	Bingo (traditional song)
op	*Hop on Pop* by Dr. Seuss

WORDS OF NOTE

"I found that just 38 phonograms with added beginning consonants can make 654 different one-syllable words. These same phonograms can be found in many polysyllabic words as well. . .With just 38 rimes students can write, spell and read over 600 relatively common one-syllable words. This is one reason to use the phonograms in the Table for reading and spelling lessons…Special spelling lessons using word lists focusing on just one or two patterns can also be effective."

—Edward Fry, "The Reading Teacher," April 1998

Examples of items on the 3D collage include:

◉ *Hop on Pop* book
◉ toy stop sign
◉ Poptarts box
◉ popcorn box
◉ lollipop bag

Explicit Teaching: Modeling Strategies Through Mini-Lessons

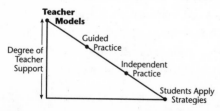

The following mini-lessons focus on strategies for transferring students' growing awareness of common word families to the actual writing process.

Lesson Focusing Question	Lesson Purpose Statement
What do good spellers do?	They notice patterns, they make connections, and they generate additional words using common word families or rimes.
How do good spellers build new words?	They add, substitute, or delete letters before common word families (i.e., cat—flat). They add, substitute, or delete letters after common word families (i.e., cat—catch).
How do good spellers write new words?	Good spellers think and say, 'What do I know about words that can help me?'
How do good spellers edit their writing?	They create lists of common word families to include in their personal dictionaries for future reference.

Mini-Lesson #1

Essential Understanding: *"What do good spellers do?"*

"They notice patterns, they make connections, and they generate additional words using common word families or rimes."

Focus of Lesson: The intent of this mini-lesson is to help children develop an awareness of common word families or rimes and how to use them to expand their spelling vocabulary.

Whole-Class Instruction: Begin by reading aloud Dr. Seuss's popular rhyming book, *Hop on Pop*. After reading the book once to expose children to the rhythm and rhyme, invite the class to listen for */op/* words used by the author. Create a word web, first listing students' discoveries, and then branching off to include additional */op/* family words. Demonstrate or model for the children how additional words may be generated by changing the onset (the letters preceding the vowel).

Introduce more challenging, multi-syllabic words by reminding students that adding common suffixes is a good way to create additional pattern words. The word webs at right nicely transfer the strategies learned in Phase Three (building words) to this phase. Display such jointly-generated word web charts in your classroom for easy reference by students.

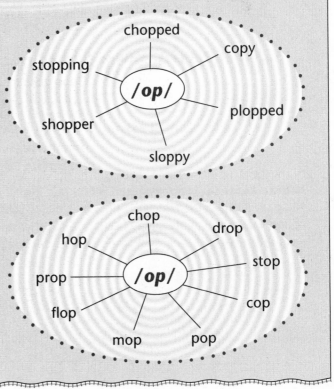

Mini-Lesson #2

Essential Understanding: *"How do good spellers build new words?"*

"They add, substitute, or delete letters before common word families (i.e., cat—flat). They add, substitute, or delete letters after common word families (i.e., cat—catch)."

Focus of Lesson: This mini-lesson provides students with further experience in building words.

Whole-Class Instruction: Invite children to come sit around the pocket chart. Ask several students to demonstrate how they can create additional pattern words by moving index cards containing consonants, blends, digraphs, and phonograms within the pocket chart.

This mini-lesson provides another good opportunity to synthesize several important spelling strategies: using common rules and applying essential spelling rules. For example, point out to students that when we add certain suffixes to rimes ending with a consonant, the consonant must be doubled (e.g., *chatting*).

Onset	Rime	Suffix
C	AT	CH
FL	AT	
TH	AT	
CH	ATT	ING

Mini-Lesson #3

Essential Understanding: *"How do good spellers write new words?"*

"Good spellers think and say, 'What do I know about words that can help me?'"

Focus of Lesson: This mini-lesson draws students' attention to using common word families to generate rhyming text innovations.

Whole-Class Instruction: Start off by reading aloud the popular rhyming text, *Oh, A-Hunting We Will Go.* Model aloud how writers may use a popular rhyming refrain to generate their own "innovations" on a text.

SAMPLE DIALOGUE:

Mrs. H.: We can go a-hunting, too. I think I will try my own new rhyme.

(Mrs. H. changes the rhyming elements in the repetitive refrain on the board or chart paper.)

TEACHER'S CORNER
Write the repetitive refrain on chart paper, leaving blank the rhyming portions that change (e.g. *goat* and *coat*) and then laminate the chart. Write the children's rhyming words on index cards and affix to the chart with tacking glue.

Mrs. H: Boys and girls, you can create your own innovations on this text by thinking of what you know about common word families. Think of the name of an animal and think of a word that rhymes with it or has the same word family *and* makes sense in this text.

(The children begin to generate a list of rhyming words to substitute in the original text. Mrs. H. lists their suggestions on the index cards.)

Mrs. H.: Who would like to come up to the chart and paste your words on our text?

Vivi: I can change this song using the words *skunk* and *trunk*.

Mrs. H.: Let's read together the innovation that Vivi just created.

Mrs. H. and class: Oh, a-hunting we will go, a-hunting we will go, we'll catch a skunk and put him in a trunk, and then we'll let him go.

(Mrs. H. continues the mini-lesson, allowing three more children to demonstrate their innovations.)

> Oh, a-hunting we will go,
> a-hunting we will go
>
> We'll catch a goat
>
> And put him in a coat
>
> And then we'll let him go.
>
> —Traditional

Mini-Lesson #4

Essential Understanding: *"How do good spellers edit their writing?"*

"They create lists of common word families to include in their personal dictionaries for future reference."

Focus of Lesson: This mini-lesson stresses how writers use many tools when revising or editing their drafts, including a dictionary, thesaurus, and/or rhyming dictionary.

Whole-Class Instruction: Invite children to dedicate a section of their own personal dictionaries to a listing of "Common Word Families," with examples. See below for a sample dictionary page.

During an interactive writing lesson, demonstrate and "share the pen" with the children, modeling how to refer to their dictionaries for assistance with spelling words containing common phonograms. For example, you might model how students can write an entry in their science journals—"Today the tadpole lost its tail."—and show them how they can spell the word *tail* by referring to the rhyming dictionary with the *ail* family words listed.

Common Word Families			
ab	crab	**ag**	bag
	lab		tag
ack	black	**ail**	tail
	track		sail

Guided Practice Activities

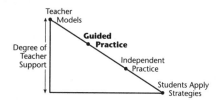

In our experience children often become comfortable generating lists of "word family" words, but do not regularly and consistently transfer this knowledge to their writing. We therefore recommend that you provide your students with ample opportunities for guided practice within the context of real writing. This section describes four contextually-based activities in which students can transfer the strategies they've learned in the mini-lessons to the writing process. The chart below provides an overview of these activities, their purpose, and the lessons they are intended to accompany.

Overview of Guided Practice Activities for Phase Four

Guided Practice Activity	Use For	Accompanies This Mini-Lesson
Word Family I Spy—Using Poems	Noticing patterns, making connections, and generating new words using common word families (rimes)	What do good spellers do?
Word Family Grids	Adding, substituting, or deleting letters before or after common word families to build new words	How do good spellers build new words?
Innovation on Text	Using known words to build new words	How do good spellers write new words?
Using personal dictionaries as a reference tool	Editing	How do good spellers edit their writing?

Guided Practice Activity: WORD FAMILY I SPY—USING POEMS

Purpose: To use common word families (rimes) to build new words

Use for: Noticing patterns, making connections, and generating new words using common word families (rimes)

Materials: Poem "Seasons" by Helen H. Moore written on chart paper; photocopy of the poem "Seasons" (see page 109) for each child

Procedure: Gather children around the easel for a demonstration lesson before giving them a copy of the poem.

SAMPLE DIALOGUE:

Mrs. M.: We are going to look at the poem "Seasons" to see if we can notice any patterns in the poem.

Sammy: There are a lot of /ot/ words.

Amanda: /ot/ is the rime.

108

Michelle: *Hot, spot,* and *not* rhyme.

Mrs. M.: All of you are right. I am going to circle all of the /ot/ words because that is the pattern that we have noticed. Now let's use this pattern to help us generate new words. Can anyone think of any other /ot/ words?

Mary: *got*

Katie: *slot*

Mrs. M.: Terrific! I am going to give each of you a copy of this poem. Circle the pattern wherever you see it and then, on a separate sheet, write as many /ot/ words as you can. We'll meet for a group share when the timer goes off.

> **SEASONS**
>
> Summer is hot.
> Winter is not.
>
> Except, that is
> if you live in a spot
> where
> Summer is cold,
> and Winter is hot!
>
> —Helen H. Moore,
> *A Poem a Day*

Guided Practice Activity: WORD FAMILY GRIDS

Purpose: To build new words from common word families

Use for: Adding, substituting, or deleting letters before or after common word families to build new words

Materials: Word family grid photocopies; easel; chart paper; marker. Prepare a word family grid (see model below) by filling in the desired word family in the center box on the grid. Copy this grid on chart paper or on an overhead transparency.

Procedure: Distribute a photocopied word grid to each child. Have the class work individually to brainstorm as many words as possible within that word family and to fill in their sheets. They can do this by adding, substituting, or deleting letters before or after common word families. Afterward, gather the children for group sharing and use your transparency or chart to fill in the words that students volunteer.

Completed Example:

Targeted word family provided for children.

c	**at**	
fl	**at**	
c	**at**	ch
r	**at**	s

Columns left blank for children to write in.

Guided Practice Activity: INNOVATION ON TEXT

Purpose: To build new words

Use for: Using known words to build new words

Materials: The book *Oh, A-Hunting We Will Go*; "Oh, A-Hunting We Will Go" photocopied sheet (see page 110)

Procedure: Gather the children and read aloud the book *Oh, A-Hunting We Will Go*. Afterward, help students to identify the rhymes and rimes on each page of the book. Then invite them to make a class book of "Oh, A-Hunting We Will Go." Have each child make his or her own page by asking them to think up and write two rimes in the spaces provided and to illustrate the bottom of the page. While the children work on their own, circulate among them, coaching as needed. When the work is completed, gather the class for a group sharing. Finally, collate the pages and bind them into a class book.

Cathryn

Oh, A-Hunting we will go,

A-Hunting we will go,

We'll catch _bananas_

and put him in _pajamas_

and then we'll let him go.

Some possibilities include:

fox - box	snake - shake
tack - backpack	dragon - wagon
car - jar	man - can
map - flap	tower - shower
mouse - house	frog - log
chip- ship	bed - shed
rat - hat	hook - book
rag - bag	mop - top

TEACHER'S CORNER
Depending on the age and ability of the children, having them brainstorm some possibilities prior to the activity may be helpful. The sillier the better!

Guided Practice Activity:
USING PERSONAL DICTIONARIES AS A REFERENCE TOOL

Purpose: To use personal dictionaries as a reference tool

Use for: Editing

Materials: Personal dictionary; white correction tape; photocopied "Word Family Story" sheet (see model below)

Procedure: Provide each child with a copy of the "Word Family Story" activity sheet. Point out which word family is being studied and explain that this word family is spelled incorrectly throughout the story. Challenge the children to fix the errors, using their personal dictionaries as a reference. Make available white correction tape, which students can use to cover the errors.

Word Family Story

It was a snowy duy tod____. I went out to pley. I was getting cold. I went inside to put on another liyer of clothes. I was still cold. The girl next door brought out a triy of hot chocolate. I had to p____ her a dime for a cup. On the wuy, I saw a cat running aw____. I picked it up and started to s____, "Is this anyone's cat?" A boy yelled, "It's mine!" We pluyed together for the rest of the duy.

Independent Practice: Learning Center Activities

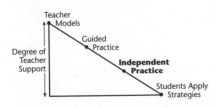

Teacher Models

Degree of Teacher Support

Guided Practice

Independent Practice

Students Apply Strategies

After the Phase Four mini-lessons and guided practice, we provide students with an opportunity to explore a range of hands-on activities that reinforce making connections, noticing patterns, and generating new words using common word families (rimes). The following four learning center activities offer young children independent practice of these word study strategies. As in the other phases, each activity includes a period of modeling and instruction—essentially, an introduction to the activity. After this introduction, place the activity into a learning center and make it available to the class.

Overview of Independent Practice Activities for Phase Four

Independent Practice Activity	Learning Style Connection	Purpose
Word Searches	Linguistic, Spatial, and Interpersonal	Good spellers notice patterns and make connections, they say "I know *hop* so I can spell *pop*."
Word Wheels	Linguistic and Spatial	Good spellers build new words.
Silly Sentences and Rhymes	Linguistic and Interpersonal	Good spellers generate new words using common word families (rimes).
Editing Word Family Text	Linguistic and Interpersonal	Good spellers use print around the room (word webs, charts, and poems) to check their spelling.

Independent Practice Activity: WORD SEARCHES

Learning Style: Linguistic, Interpersonal, and Spatial

Purpose: To notice patterns and make connections among words. Good spellers say, "I know *hop* so I can spell *pop*."

Materials: Word search grids (see model on page 112); pencils and crayons; clear plastic sheet sleeves; dry erase markers

Modeling and Introduction: By this point in the school year the children have done a number of word searches and they are familiar with the concept and process. Explain to them that now they will make word searches for their classmates using the word family rimes that were the focus of the guided practice lesson. As a reminder, show students a sample of a completed word search. Alternately, if children need more experience, work with the class to circle words in an already-constructed word search.

Name _____

Spelling Word Study Strategy

Challenge! Make a Word Search for your friends to solve.
Use as many spelling wordes as you can.

Rules: Only go down or across.

Try to find:

Solving a friend's word search is a fun way for children to recognize word patterns.

Learning Center Activity: Have children work in pairs to write down some of the word family words on the lines provided on the word search sheet. Ask them to work together to write the letters in the boxes of the grid to form the words on their list—one letter per box, with words only going up or down. When each pair has completed the word search, have them slip it in a clear plastic sleeve and try to find the words they have written by taking turns circling them with a dry erase marker. If their word search works, they can erase the circles with a tissue and give it to two other children at their table to try. The word searches can then be stored and offered later to children to use during choice time.

TEACHER'S CORNER

Children love to solve each other's word searches. We have them make word searches with their families as part of their Home Links work, and then ask them to bring these to school for their classmates to try. You can also make a class book of word searches. Make sure you put each in a clear plastic sleeve so it can be done many times.

Independent Practice Activity: WORD WHEELS

Learning Style: Linguistic and Spatial

Purpose: Building new words. Good spellers learn to generate words using the common word family or rime to make word wheel games.

Materials: Word wheel mat (see model on page 113); pencils: colored markers; paper fasteners; scissors

Modeling and Introduction: The teacher tells the whole class that they will be making word family wheels today. She begins by holding up a completed word wheel and asking for a volunteer to explain how partners could work together to use the wheel.

SAMPLE DIALOGUE:

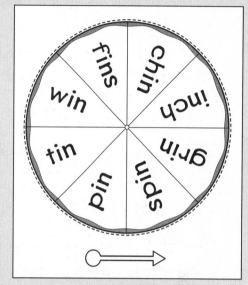

Sara: I say a word or finger-spell it using the sign language alphabet chart and you have to make the spinner go to that word on the wheel.

Paul: You could also spin to a word on the wheel and ask your partner to finger spell it or to give you another word from that word family.

Ms. K.: Those are both great ideas. Now you'll be working in centers to make your word wheels.

Learning Center Activity: Have students work in pairs at four learning center tables. Ask each child to make two word wheels using the word family words—one to take home for practice and one to keep in school for playing games. After they fill in the words, have students cut out the word circle and the spinner and attach the spinner with a paper fastener. Some children will need help attaching the spinner with a fastener. (It's a good idea to have a parent or other volunteer help with this activity.) After their word wheels are finished, ask children to make up their own games to play with their partner. (Note: It's a good idea to laminate the wheel that is going to stay in school. If you do plan to laminate, collect those word wheels before children cut out the circles and attach the fasteners. Have them finish construction on another day.)

Independent Practice Activity: SILLY SENTENCES AND RHYMES

Learning Style: Linguistic and Interpersonal

Purpose: Generating new words using common word families (rimes). Good spellers notice patterns and make connections.

Materials: Copies of poem "Higglety, Pigglety, Pop!" (see page 68) (use a different poem for each weekly word family); lined paper at each center with room for drawings; pencils; crayons

Modeling and Introduction: Remind children of how they played "I Spy" during the guided practice lesson, noticing patterns and word families in poems.

SAMPLE DIALOGUE:

Ms. K.: Today we'll use a funny poem, "Higglety, Pigglety, Pop!" and change the rimes to make a new silly sentence. (*Ms. K. gives out copies of the poem, one to every two children, and the class reads it together out loud. Ms. K. invites the children to think of other word substitutions using the /op/ rime pattern. She starts the line from the poem, "The dog has eaten the _____.")*

Claire: The dog has eaten the top!

Jose: The mouse has nibbled at my crop! *(The children continue to offer other word substitutions using the /op/ rime and other words to change the meaning of the poem.)*

Ms. K.: You have great ideas for silly sentences using the /op/ words. Let's see if you can work with a partner to write a silly sentence for the /op/ words, change the meaning of the poem, and draw a funny picture to go with your idea.

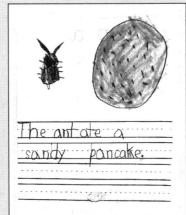

The ant ate a
sandy pancake.

Learning Center Activity: Have students work in pairs at four learning center tables. Ask each child in a pair to make his or her own silly sentence, and then to read and show it to the partner. Alternately, have one child write the sentence and the partner illustrate it.

TEACHER'S CORNER: Management Tip

Have the partners read their silly sentences and show their pictures to the whole class during group sharing time. Later, make a "Silly Sentence" class book and invite the children to take turns bringing it home to share with their families.

Independent Practice Activity: EDITING WORD FAMILY TEXT

Learning Style: Linguistic and Interpersonal

Purpose: To use personal dictionaries, word webs, charts, and poems to edit one's own written work.

Materials: Copies of uncorrected student Spelling Challenge assessment sentences; copies of Silly Sentence or stories that have been written for Home Links; yellow highlight markers or "boo-boo" tape (wide-size white correction tape)

Modeling and Introduction: The teacher begins by telling students that today they will use student work to practice editing. (Note: Be sure to get the permission ahead of time from a child whose work will be used as a sample.)

SAMPLE DIAGLOGUE:

Ms. K.: Today we will edit a writing sample using our personal dictionaries, word family webs, and poetry charts around the room. What will we look for?

Rahul: We'll check our personal dictionaries and class poems to see if the word family words are spelled correctly. We'll check sight words from the word wall and check class charts to see if we have followed the spelling rules.

John: It's a good idea to work with a partner so that we can help each other. We can use our "boo-boo" tape to write the corrections after we have highlighted the words that need correction.

Miranda: *Everybody makes mistakes, even grown-ups. You learn from your mistakes.*

Learning Center Activity: Divide the children into groups and give every two children a piece of writing to edit (either their own or another student's). Circulate among the groups answering questions and giving guidance where needed. Afterward, during sharing circle, it is important to make a list of the errors that students noticed during their editing so that these word study skills may be reinforced.

TEACHER'S CORNER
Children enjoy wearing simple paper bands that say "Editor at Work" as they work in their groups.

Teacher Assessment of Student Learning

Through ongoing observation and classroom-based specific assessments, teachers continue to collect data that reflect students expanding spelling vocabularies.

ONGOING ASSESSMENT

During this phase, teachers' kid-watching focuses on assessing students' ability to notice patterns, make connections, and generate additional words using common word families or rimes. For example, during guided and independent practice activities, teachers use the observations log to record successes and confusions as students apply their knowledge of common word families. (See pages 47–48 for recommendations about how to set up and manage the log.)

SPECIFIC CLASSROOM-BASED ASSESSMENTS

In order to more formally evaluate individual students' acquisition and application of word families and connections among words, we recommend using the following three classroom-based assessment tools.

- ⊚ **Buddy Spelling Checks:** Ask spelling partners to dictate 5–10 word family pattern words to each other and check their partner's accuracy.

- ⊚ **Contextual Dictation:** Dictate five sentences to small groups or the whole class.

- ⊚ **Student Writing Sample:** Select four writing samples from students' journals to evaluate their application of the strategies learned during this phase.

Buddy Spelling Checks

Using a teacher-prepared list of 5–10 words composed from the targeted word family, students use chalkboard slates or paper to "test" their partners. This is illustrated in the sample on page 116.

Contextual Dictation

Dictate five sentences to small groups or the whole class. Since this is the final phase of the spelling/word study approach, the sentences should include words that reflect strategies covered in all four phases. These sentences thus include targeted sight words, words with

Buddy Check

1. Your Buddy reads your words to you and you write them in the first column.
2. Together you check to see if they are correct.
3. If you didn't spell a word right, write it correctly in the last column.
4. Highlight or circle parts you want to remember and make the word with magnetic letters.

Word

Correct Spelling
(Highlight or circle the part you want to remember.)

_____   _____

_____   _____

_____   _____

_____   _____

_____   _____

_____   _____

_____   _____

_____   _____

prefixes and/or suffixes, compound words, and words with common rimes. After completing the dictation, encourage students to generate as many words as they can from the word family covered that week. Be sure to remind students to edit their sentences for both spelling and punctuation errors.

Student Writing Samples

Collect final writing samples from student journal entries to assess students' independent application of learned strategies. We recommend that you conference with students so that you can evaluate their spelling progress jointly. You might opt to share and compare all four writing samples so that students can see evidence of growth as they celebrate their spelling successes.

Sample Phase Four Dictation
/ay/

1. The cats like playing in the basement or attic.
2. The man chats to his buddies on the subway.
3. The queen said to put the crayons away.
4. Today all of the snow will be plowed away.
5. There is a layer of hay in the barn for the animals.

Final Thoughts

As we come to the end of our four-year journey in writing this book, we all exhale a sigh of contentment. As we have watched one student after another grow into proficient spellers over the past few years, we have felt proud and fulfilled as educators. We believe that the research we have done for this book has given our students the best advantage in spelling. We can only hope that students like Kelsey, who were so bored and bothered by mindless spelling activities, will become excited and empowered to tackle new word study challenges with this approach.

As educators and literacy advocates, we classroom teachers need to make sure that each and every word study activity we create for our students has meaning. We don't want children to just memorize words for weekly spelling tests; we want them to be able to use the words they learn in their daily writing. The goal of any successful spelling program is a transfer of knowledge to every aspect of the curriculum. If students can spell a word for their spelling test, we want them to be able to spell it in math, science, and during Writer's Workshop. As you make this word study approach your own, remember: spelling is not a memorization of weekly spelling words, it is a process of figuring out language, just like speaking and reading, and you are the facilitator.

HOME LINKS

Independent Application: Home Link Extensions

Home Links are activities that provide children with additional opportunities to practice and review effective word-solving strategies outside of the classroom. Parents and family members can use these innovative activities to support the early spelling efforts of children.

Each of the Home Link activities, which the children bring home to share with their families, is a new version of an activity they have already learned and practiced in class. Bringing a familiar activity home and involving the family in it both reinforces children's knowledge and allows them to experience that knowledge in a different situation. Through these activities, children become more comfortable playing and experimenting with words. Our goal here, as throughout the program, is to encourage young students to look at words, to listen to words, and to manipulate words in as many settings as possible.

The Home Links portion of our spelling program highlights the following aspects of word study:

⊙ **In Phase One,** the children "learn how to learn," or memorize the spelling of sight words. For example, in a Phase One Home Link, the children learn that sight words are embedded in meaningful contexts—the word *the* in the phrase "the house." Students study a sight word by rebuilding it using letter cards and then locating the targeted sight words in story texts. (Refer to the mini-lesson for introducing sight words, page 26.)

   Celebrating words through poetry is an important part of early word study. In one Phase One Home Link, children find and circle all "target words" studied in weekly word study. They are encouraged to use word-solving strategies to read the poems and enjoy the rhythm of the word patterns. (See the parent letter for Phase I: Learning Sight Words: Visual and Auditory Sequencing Strategies, later in this Appendix.)

⊙ Home Link activities in **Phase Two** focus on developing phonological skills by having children work with rhyming and phoneme manipulation. Parents are encouraged to sing song games with rhyming patterns and read rhyming poetry at home.

   In one Phase Two Home Link, Mystery Bag Rhymes, each child receives a bag to take home and fill with two rhyming objects (i.e., a block and a sock). The children then bring their objects to school for show and tell. During the sharing, they hold up one object and ask their classmates to predict what the rhyming mystery object might be. If the children cannot find rhyming objects at home, they can bring in two rhyming pictures or words on index cards to share.

   Another Home Link activity for Phase Two is the Rhyme Time Link. In this activity, children draw or paste pictures of rhyming words in boxes. They label the pictures and bring them to school for weekly word study. The pages can be bound together to create a class book for the word study center. For an added challenge, a flap can be added over one of the pictures on each page. Children can guess the rhyme and lift the flap to see if their prediction was correct.

   In yet another Home Link activity for Phase Two, the Word Detective Link, children revisit poetry and highlight rhyming words.

- In **Phase Three** Home Link activities, children use visual, auditory, and meaning features of known words to make new words. They work with their letter cards once again to build new words from known words. For example, they can build onto the word *cat*. By changing the ending sound, they can make *catch*, *can*, *cap*, etc. Through these activities, children learn to manipulate letters to make new words.

- By **Phase Four,** children have seen the patterns of words, heard the sounds of words, learned to manipulate these sounds to make new words, and can build on all of this knowledge to use known words to spell new words. In this phase, children use common word families to increase their spelling repertoire and they complete weekly spelling Home Link activities like Look, Say, Copy; Silly Sentences; and Word Search. Establishing a routine by assigning the same Home Link each day of the week is useful in this phase. For example, the children might complete Look, Say, Copy on Mondays; Silly Sentences on Tuesdays; and Word Search on Wednesdays.

Remember, Home Links are a way for children to practice the spelling strategies they are learning in their own personal environment. Our goal in this program is for children to gain the ability to spell for the weekly spelling challenge, and also be able to spell words correctly in their journals, on grocery lists, and in letters. We want them to be able to recognize small words inside of big words and to constantly make connections among words. This will enable them to not only become proficient spellers, but also proficient readers and writers.

Letters to the Children and to Parents About Home Links

In this section you will find several brief letters to the children and several longer ones to the parents. You might use these letters as models for your own.

The parent letters are particularly important. You may want to hand out the letters at Back to School or Open House night, or send them home as you enter each phase of the spelling program. They allow parents and family members the opportunity to become involved in their children's spelling progress. At the same time, they provide a little background as to why you are teaching spelling this way.

SAMPLE LETTERS TO STUDENTS

Date: _____

Dear Girls and Boys,

This week our sharing will focus on phonemic awareness. Please bring an item (or drawing of something) that belongs to the _____ word family.

Date: _____

Dear Girls and Boys,

This week our sharing will focus on the number of syllables (or parts) in a word. Please bring an object (or draw a picture of an item) whose name has _____ parts (syllables) in it.

Date: _____

Dear Girls and Boys,

This week our sharing will focus on rhyming words. Please bring two objects or a drawing of two things that rhyme.

SAMPLE LETTERS TO PARENTS

Introductory Letter

Dear Parents,

Research tells us that children who are encouraged to listen for sounds within words and represent these sounds as approximate spellings will begin to formulate and refine ideas about spelling in the same way they formulate and refine their spoken language. This is what we will be working toward during our time together in the classroom. The children will be given the opportunity to experiment with spelling. Their approximate spellings are learners' attempts to find patterns and order in the spelling system. For this reason, the spelling program we will be using highlights those patterns in language. We will focus on sight words and/or word families each week. We introduce these words and patterns to the children informally during mini-lessons, in guided reading groups, journals, and centers. This is done in order to make a smooth transition into the spelling program.

There are two things necessary to be a good speller of the English language: auditory sequencing and visual memory. Auditory sequencing is the ability to listen for the sequence of sounds in words. Children will learn how to make the transition from sounds to letters as they engage in journal and modeled writing activities in the classroom. Visual memory is the ability to focus on the way words look. Once children have been exposed to modeling of standard spelling through environmental print, classroom story charts, Big Books, and literature, we draw their attention to the visual features of words. For example, some words have a silent e at the end (as in the word cake), or a y that makes an e sound (as in the word happy). At this point, children begin to memorize several high-frequency vocabulary words.

Your help at home with the Home Links portion of our spelling program is key to the success of your child as a speller. I will be sending Home Link worksheets home for your child to practice spelling strategies, to practice playing with words, and to practice building his or her repertoire of known words.

The purpose of our spelling program is to foster an interest in written language and to begin to teach strategies that all competent spellers employ. Good spellers are not afraid to take risks, so please encourage your children to write for many purposes—have them write grocery lists, phone message, letters, and stories. Point out words in your child's environment. Open his or her eyes to the words around us.

Thank you for your support and involvement in your child's education.

Sincerely,
Your child's teacher

Phase One Letter

Dear Parents,

    As we begin to experiment and play with the words around us in school, you can play a key role through the Home Links portion of our spelling program. Over the next few weeks, we will be concentrating on learning a core of sight vocabulary words. After learning these 25 targeted sight words, we will then build on what your child knows to learn more words.

    Throughout this process, your help at home is integral to your child's success as a speller. I will be sending home letter cards for your child to use to build his or her words. Your child will learn these sight words at school, as they are embedded in meaningful texts (i.e., books read for read aloud or in reading groups.) He or she will study the sight words by rebuilding them using the letter cards and then locating the targeted sight words in story texts.

    Children will then bring home letter cards and practice sheets. Please ask your child to find the targeted words in the books he or she reads at home, on signs, in stores, and anywhere you see these words in their environment. Children should then practice building the words with their letter cards and write them on the practice sheet.

    I will also be sending home poems for your child to read with you. Encourage him or her to find the sight words in the poems as you read them together.

    Enjoy all of the activities you do together at home—your enthusiasm for these activities is contagious. Thank you for your support and involvement in your child's education.

Sincerely,
Your child's teacher

Phase Two Letter

Dear Parents,

    As we enter Phase Two of our word study program, we will be experimenting with poems and songs. In class, we will be singing songs with rhyming patterns and reading poems with rhyming patterns. These songs and poems provide opportunities to play with words and experiment with patterns of the English language. Feel free to dive in and play some of the song games learned in school at home or in the car.

    By participating in the Home Link activities for this phase, you can create even more opportunities for furthering your child's learning through word play and experimentation. One Home Link activity your child will be asked to complete is Mystery Bag Rhymes. In this activity, your child should find two rhyming items (such as a hat and a bat), and place them in a bag to bring to school for show and tell. Other Home Link activities, like the Rhyme Time Link, will revisit our poetry to highlight rhyming words within the poems.

    This is a fun and exciting time in your child's education. Enjoy their enthusiasm for words and play along with him or her. Thank you again for your continued support and involvement in your child's education.

Sincerely,
Your child's teacher

Phase Three Letter

Dear Parents,

    Over the past few weeks, your child has been adding many new sight words to his or her repertoire of known words. During the next phase of word study, Phase Three, we will be building on the knowledge your child has gained. For example, if your child knows how to spell *the*, he or she can build the words *then*, *there*, *they*, and *their*.

    Your child will once again be using letter cards to build known words and then to build new words. As always, look for these old and new words in your child's environment at home and in your everyday living.

    You are probably finding that your child is noticing print everywhere you go. This is an exciting time for children—a whole new world of words is opening up to them. They are beginning to find little words they already know inside bigger words, which is a natural progression of this stage of their development. Please encourage this, and praise their attempts at making meaning of print.

    As always, thank you for your support and encouragement in your child's education.

Sincerely,
Your child's teacher

Phase Four Letter

Dear Parents,

    What are the characteristics of a good speller? Good spellers can hear sounds and recognize patterns in language, they can manipulate these sounds to make words, they have a heightened auditory awareness of words, they have a heightened visual awareness of words, and they can use a known word to spell an unknown word.

    We have been working in our classroom to reach these goals. In the next phase of our learning process, your child will be using all of his or her knowledge of words to build an even larger repertoire of words. Your child will be completing several Home Link activities each week. Below is an explanation of each activity I will ask him or her to complete at home, together with you.

Look, Say, Copy

    This is a spelling strategy based on research in the field of spelling education. This is not an activity in which your child writes spelling words three times over. Here's how this important procedure works:

    Your child will write his or her first spelling word in the LOOK column. Then he or she looks at the word and says the sounds of the word. This is done so that the child can hear and visualize the word at the same time. Be sure your child is saying the sounds of the word, and not the letters (*k* at instead of *c-a-t*). He or she should then cover the word by folding the paper on the dotted line and rewrite it while saying the sounds. This allows your child to recall the visual pattern of the word as he or she says the word. Lastly, your child should check to make sure he or she spelled the word correctly by uncovering the first column and comparing the words. If the word was spelled correctly, a check should be placed in the CHECK column. If it was spelled incorrectly, the child should write it one more time in that column, saying the sounds while writing the word.

Word Search

We will also be completing a word search. The purpose of this Home Link is for your child to play a game using his or her spelling words. Your child should hide the spelling words inside the boxes of the word search and fill in the rest of the boxes with random letters. Remember, your child may add other words from the same spelling family if he or she likes. The next day, when your child brings his or her completed word search to school, it will be traded for another child's. The two will then complete each other's word search.

Silly Sentence

Another weekly Home Link activity is writing a silly sentence. This assignment was designed to be a fun activity for you and your child to work on together. I do not want any child to dread spelling homework, so please have fun with this activity and be as creative as you can.

The goal for this Home Link is for your child to play with the spelling family being studied and find patterns in the English language. He or she should first generate a list of words from the spelling family; these might be spelling words or just words that are in the family. (Remember, the goal is to recognize patterns in spelling.) Then encourage your child to use some of the words in a silly sentence or story and draw a picture to accompany the sentence or story. We will then share these sentences in class.

Through all of these Home Link activities, your child should become comfortable playing and experimenting with words. Our goal is for our students to manipulate words, listen to words, and look at words in order to become good spellers.

Thank you again for your continued support and involvement in your child's education.

Sincerely,
Your child's teacher

SAMPLE HIGH-FREQUENCY READERS

This reader highlights the high-frequency words *me* and *my*.

Swing, swing, swing.

3

My swing is so big
I'll get my frog.

4

My frog will swing with me.

5

124

This reader highlights the high-frequency word *like*.

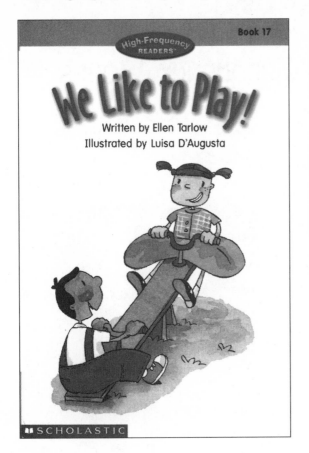

What do you like to do?
I like to draw.

2

What do you like to do?
I like to dig.

3

What do you like to do?
I like to pull.

4

ONE HUNDRED HIGH-FREQUENCY WORDS

a	don't	look	the
after	for	make	their
all	from	man	them
am	get	me	then
an	go	mother	there
and	going	my	they
are	had	no	this
as	has	not	to
asked	have	now	too
at	he	of	two
away	her	on	up
back	here	one	us
be	him	or	very
because	his	our	was
before	how	out	we
big	I	over	went
but	I'm	play	were
by	if	put	what
came	in	said	when
can	into	saw	where
come	is	see	who
could	it	she	will
day	just	so	with
did	like	than	you
do	little	that	your

(Source: Pinnell, H.S, and I.C. Fountas. *Word Matters: Teaching Phonics and Spelling in the Reading/Writing Classroom*. Portsmouth, NH: Heinemann, 1998.)

Spelling Success in the Early Grades ● Scholastic Teaching Resources

Selected Children's Literature

Dr. Seuss. *There's a Wocket in My Picket! A Book of Ridiculous Rhymes.* New York: Random House, 1974.

Dr. Seuss. *Mr. Brown Can Moo! Can You?* New York: Random House, 1970.

Dr. Seuss. *Dr. Seuss's ABC.* New York: Random House, 1963.

Dr. Seuss. *Green Eggs and Ham.* New York: Random House, 1988.

Dr. Seuss. *Horton Hatches an Egg.* New York: Random House, 1940, 1968.

Dr. Seuss. *Hop on Pop.* New York: Random House, 1963.

Dr. Seuss. *The Cat in the Hat.* New York: Random House, 1957.

Dr. Seuss. *Foxs in Socks.* New York: Random House, 1993.

Eagle, Kin. *It's Raining, It's Pouring.* Dallas, TX: Whispering Coyote Press, 1995.

Hawkins, Colin and Jacqui Hawkins. *Jen the Hen's Big Book.* Place: Dorling Kindersley Publishing, 1983.

Hawkins, Colin and Jacqui Hawkins. *Mig the Pig's Big Book.* New York: Dorling Kindersley Publishing, 1983.

Hawkins, Colin and Jacqui Hawkins. *Pat the Cat's Big Book.* New York: Dorling Kindersley Publishing, 1983.

Hawkins, Colin and Jacqui Hawkins. *Tog the Dog's Big Book.* New York: Dorling Kindersley Publishing, 1983.

Hawkins, Colin and Jacqui Hawkins. *Zug the Bug's Big Book.* New York: Dorling Kindersley Publishing, 1983.

Kirk, David. *Little Miss Spider.* New York: Scholastic Inc.,1999.

Martin, Bill, Jr. and John Archambault. *Chicka Chicka Boom Boom.* New York: Simon and Schuster, Inc., 1989.

Perkins, Al. *Hand, Hand, Finger, Thumb.* New York: Random House, 1969.

Steer, Dug. *Super Snappy ABC.* Brookfield, CT: The Millbrook Press, 2000.

Tarlow, Ellen. *We Like to Play!* New York: Scholastic Inc. 2000.

Trapani, Iza. *Twinkle, Twinkle, Little Star.* Dallas, TX: Whispering Coyote Press, 1994.

Trapani, Iza. *The Itsy Bitsy Spider.* Dallas, TX: Whispering Coyote Press, 1995.

Tuchman, Gail. *Swing, Swing, Swing.* New York: Scholastic Inc., 1994.

REFERENCES

Adams, Marilyn Jager, et. al. "The Elusive Phoneme." *American Educator,* Spring/summer (1998).

Beringer, Virginia W., et. al. *Learning Disability Quarterly,* Spring 2000.

Bryant, P.E. EducationNews.org. 1990.

Carlisle, Ashby. "Using Multiple Intelligences Theory To Assess Early Childhood Curricula." *Young Child,* Vol. 56, No. 6. (2001), pp. 77-83.

Clay, Marie. *Reading Recovery: A Guidebook for Teachers in Training,* Reading Recovery Early Intervention Program, 1993.

Cunningham, P.M. *Phonics They Use and Words for Reading and Writing.* New York: Harper Collins College Publishing, 1995.

Cunningham, P.M. and Cunningham, J.W. "Making Words: Enhancing the Invented Spelling–Decoding Connection." *The Reading Teacher,* Vol. 46, No. 2. (1992), p. 106.

Cunningham, P.M., Dorothy Hall and Cheryl Sigmon. *The Teacher's Guide to the Four Block Multimethod, Multilevel Framework for Grades 1-3.* Carson-Dellosa Publishing Company, 2001.

Fountas, I.C. and G.S. Pinnell. *Guided Reading: Good First Teaching For All Children.* Portsmouth, NH: Heinemann, 1996.

Fry, Edward. "The Most Common Phonograms." *The Reading Teacher,* Vol. 51, No. 7 (1998).

Fry, Fountoukidis, and Polk (1985), as referenced in Patricia M. Cunningham, *Phonics They Use and Words for Reading and Writing.* New York: Harper Collins College Publishing, 1995.

Gardner, Howard. *Frames of Mind: The Theory of Multiple Intelligences.* New York: Basic Books, 1993.

Gentry, Richard and Jean Wallace Gillet. *Teaching Kids to Spell.* Portsmouth, NH: Heinemann, 1993.

Goodman, Yetta (1979) as referenced in Burns, Roe, Ross: *Teaching Reading in Today's Elementary Schools,* 7/e. Boston: Houghton Mifflin Company, 1999.

Hempenstall, Kerry. "Phonemic Awareness: What Does It Mean?" EducationNews.org, 1998.

Nation, Kate and Charles Hulme. "Phonemic Segmentation, Not Onset-Rhyme Segmentation, Predicts Early Reading and Spelling Skills." *Reading Recovery Quarterly,* Vol. 32, No 2. (1997), pp. 154-167.

Pearson, David P., Gradual Release of Responsibility Model, Gallagher and Pearson as referenced in Keene and Zimmermann, *Mosaic of Thought: Teaching Comprehension in a Reader's Workshop.* Portsmouth, NH: Heinemann, 1983.

Pinnell, H.S. and I.C. Fountas. *Word Matters: Teaching Phonics and Spelling in the Reading/Writing Classroom.* Portsmouth, NH: Heinemann, 1998.

Templeton, Shane. *Children's Literacy: Contexts for Meaningful Learning.* Boston: Houghton Mifflin Company, 1995.